KINGDOM OVER CULTURE

Restoring Biblical Leadership in a Secularized Church

MEREDITH JAMES

Nagiyd Media

ISBN: 979-8-9928393-0-2

Unless otherwise noted, all scripture references are from the ESV (English Standard Version).

Cover and interior design by Skillhouse Studio
Photo used with permission - Mauritshuis, The Hague

Printed in the United States of America

For general inquiries or permissions related to the book, please contact:
Meredith James at meredith@drmeredithjames.com

10 9 8 7 6 5 4 3 2 1

The Lord is my Shepherd—glory belongs to Him alone.

CONTENTS

THE TRUE KING AND HIS KINGDOM

Recently, I had the opportunity to visit Buckingham Palace, a place renowned for its splendor and deep-rooted symbolism of power and authority. As I walked through its ornate halls, admiring the gilded ceilings, priceless artwork, and majestic decor, I couldn't help but feel the overwhelming sense of grandeur designed to glorify a human monarch. Every inch of the palace exudes opulence, meant to elevate the stature of a king and his kingdom—a striking display of worldly influence and prestige. But as impressive as it was, it also brought to mind a sobering reflection: this earthly magnificence, though captivating, represents a counterfeit kingdom compared to the eternal kingdom of God. This realization not only underscored the fleeting nature of human power but also mirrored how, in many ways, the church today has built its own version of such kingdoms—counterfeit structures that glorify man instead of God.

The grandeur and opulence of places like Buckingham Palace, with their lavish decorations, towering rooms, and intricate designs, serve to glorify a counterfeit king and a counterfeit kingdom. Every detail of such palaces—the golden embellishments, the meticulously crafted interiors, and the imposing architecture—exists to impress and elevate the earthly monarchs they enshrine. While awe-inspiring, these symbols of power and human achievement are ultimately fleeting. The legacy of these worldly kingdoms is built on status, wealth, and influence—things that will pass away.

In contrast, God's people are called to be part of a true kingdom with a true King, one not marked by material wealth or the fleeting admiration of men but by righteousness, humility, and eternal purpose. The kingdom of God stands in stark opposition to the glittering, empty splendor of worldly kingdoms. And yet, much like the artificial majesty of places like Buckingham Palace, many church leaders today have constructed their own versions of counterfeit kingdoms—systems built around personal fame, influence, and success. These structures, designed to glorify individuals rather than God, have diverted attention from the true King and His eternal kingdom.

To understand the kingdom of God is to understand Jesus, for the two are inseparably linked. Jesus is the kingdom of God incarnate—He didn't merely speak about the kingdom; He embodied it in everything He did. In His very being, Jesus revealed the nature of God's reign through His life of humility, service, and obedience to the

Father. His teachings, miracles, and ultimate sacrifice were all expressions of the kingdom breaking into the world. To know Christ is to know the kingdom and to live in His kingdom is to walk in His ways. Sadly, the church has often separated this understanding, treating the kingdom as an abstract concept while failing to reflect the life of Christ in leadership and ministry.

This book addresses a critical issue: the church's tendency to drift toward building these counterfeit kingdoms. Church leaders have often adopted worldly values, allowing power, influence, and growth to define success rather than faithfulness to Christ. The true kingdom of God calls for a radically different way of living and leading, one grounded in Christ's example of humility, service, and love. It is time for the church to reject the allure of secular success and return to the principles of the kingdom of God, where leadership is marked by servanthood, sacrifice, and submission to the true King.

In these pages, you will explore the ways in which church leadership culture has been influenced by the surrounding world and challenged to reorient toward Christ and His mission. The message is clear: the mistakes of the past don't have to dictate the future, but change will only come if pastors and ministry leaders realign themselves with God's kingdom. The kingdom of God is not about grandiose structures or personal glory. It is about advancing God's eternal reign with integrity, humility, and a deep commitment to Christ's teachings.

The call is urgent. The world doesn't need more counterfeit kingdoms; it needs the church to rise up and reflect the true kingdom of God. Let this book serve as a guide and a challenge to all who are ready to abandon the imitation and embrace the reality of life under the true King, Jesus Christ.

Chapter One

THE CHURCH'S LEADERSHIP DILEMMA

Navigating Secularization and Reclaiming Biblical Principles

IN RECENT YEARS, the church has reached a critical juncture, where the principles of secular culture and business practices have begun to infiltrate and influence the way ministry is conducted. Leadership within the kingdom of God, however, is distinct and must be rooted firmly in the spiritual principles laid out in scripture. While secular leadership strategies can offer helpful tools, they should never become the guiding force for the church.

The growing tension between worldly influence and biblical leadership is evident across churches of all sizes and traditions. Many churches, in an effort to remain culturally relevant, have embraced methods that prioritize growth, entertainment, and branding over discipleship, holiness, and spiritual depth. As society continues to shift toward consumerism, entertainment-driven engagement, and corporate-style strategies, church leaders face increasing pressure to adopt secular models of success. The temptation to conform—measuring effectiveness by numbers, visibility, and cultural relevance—can be strong. However, scripture calls church leaders to a different standard.

Rather than mirroring societal trends, they must anchor themselves in biblical truth, prioritizing spiritual transformation over external recognition. True kingdom leadership is not about adapting to culture but about shaping it through steadfast devotion to Christ. Scripture makes the answer clear: God's leaders are not called to reflect the culture but to embody Christ. Leadership in His kingdom is not measured by popularity, numbers, or public approval but by faithfulness, humility, and obedience to His Word. The church's effectiveness is not found in adopting secular models of success but in embracing the countercultural, transformative power of Christ-centered leadership.

THE INFILTRATION OF SECULAR METHODS IN CHURCH LEADERSHIP

The secularization of church leadership has become a concerning trend, particularly in megachurches, seeker-sensitive movements, and churches shaped by the church growth philosophy. In an effort to stay relevant and attract new members, many pastors and church leaders have embraced secular methods that prioritize rapid expansion over discipleship. While these strategies may generate impressive numerical growth, they often fail to cultivate spiritually mature believers who are deeply rooted in Christ. As a result, churches risk becoming consumer-driven organizations rather than discipleship-centered communities.

This shift toward a consumer-driven approach has transformed some churches into entities more focused on material success than fostering deep, transformative relationships with God. Leadership conferences and church growth seminars frequently emphasize branding, marketing strategies, and audience engagement—concepts borrowed directly from corporate America. Although these tools are not inherently wrong, when they become the driving force behind ministry decisions the church drifts away from its God-ordained purpose.

The impact of secular culture on the church has been profound. Many leaders, often unknowingly, have allowed business models and cultural trends to shape their ministries. Church leadership, once defined by servanthood and faithfulness, is now often measured by platforms and social media reach. As a result, the emphasis has shifted toward numbers, celebrity status, and outward success rather than on the spiritual health and faithfulness of the congregation.

The consequences of this shift are clear in the increasing number of ministry failures, scandals, and the overall weakening of the church's spiritual influence. The rise and fall of high-profile pastors have revealed the dangers of leadership built on charisma rather than character. When leaders seek influence over intimacy with God, they lose sight of their divine calling.

THE URGENCY OF RECLAIMING BIBLICAL LEADERSHIP

Reclaiming biblical principles in church leadership is not just important; it's urgent. Christ's teachings, especially those related to kingdom leadership, must once again serve as the foundation for guiding the church. Pastors and ministry leaders are called to be ambassadors of Christ, reflecting His character and methods in every aspect of leadership.

This commitment requires a focus on spiritual growth rather than numerical growth, faithfulness rather than fame, and biblical truth over cultural relevance. Churches must prioritize discipleship, biblical teaching, and authentic community over polished presentations and entertainment-driven services. When the church aligns with kingdom values, it regains its power to transform lives.

In navigating the challenges of secularization, leaders need practical tools and perspectives to stay true to the mission God has entrusted to them. They must discern where cultural adaptation is appropriate and where it compromises the integrity of the gospel. Moving forward means realigning with the kingdom of God, where leadership is defined by faithfulness to Christ and His teachings—not the metrics of worldly success.

THE DANGERS OF SECULAR INFLUENCE ON CHURCH LEADERSHIP

The church and its leadership should always be guided by the spiritual principles provided by God in scripture. Leadership in the kingdom of God is fundamentally different from secular models found in culture or business. While business practices may provide useful insights, they should not drive how the church operates. When church leadership begins to resemble a corporation, it risks prioritizing marketing strategies and programs over the principles of God's Word, which are vital for fostering genuine spiritual growth.

As churches strive to maintain cultural relevance, many have unknowingly drifted into secularization. This trend is especially prevalent in large, attractional churches and those influenced by modern church growth strategies. In their pursuit of innovation and expansion, many pastors and ministry leaders have shifted their focus from biblical shepherding to business-driven leadership models. Over time, these methods redefine success—not by faithfulness to God's Word, but by attendance numbers, branding, and engagement metrics.

J.B. Watson Jr. and Walter H. Scalen Jr., in their article "'Dining with the Devil': The Unique Secularization of American Evangelical Churches," describe secularization as the process by which religion loses its influence in society, replaced by material success and pragmatic concerns.[1] This shift leads to a consumer-driven ministry model where elements of corporate culture, self-improvement ideologies, and pop-culture trends take over. When the church begins to function as a business rather than as the body of Christ, its ability to shape individual behavior and influence culture in ways that reflect the kingdom of God is diminished.

Alan Wolfe, professor of political science and director of the Boisi Center for Religion and American Public Life at Boston College, observes that "In every aspect of the religious life, American faith has met American culture— and American culture has triumphed."[2] This triumph of culture over faith is detrimental to the church, yet many evangelical churches continue down this path. Dr. Tracy Munsil of the Cultural Research Center at Arizona Christian University points to this concern in her article, "US Christians Embrace Secularism in 'Post-Christian' America," highlighting how many American churches are abandoning biblical truth and traditional theological beliefs in favor of secular cultural values.[3]

This shift is further underscored by research from Dr. George Barna's American World Inventory 2020. His findings reveal that secularism is increasingly infiltrating evangelical churches, with 52% of evangelicals rejecting absolute moral truth, 61% not reading the Bible daily, and 75% believing in humanity's basic goodness over the biblical view of sin. These statistics demonstrate that a significant portion of evangelicals are adopting beliefs and behaviors that run counter to biblical teachings and longstanding evangelical principles.[4] This trend indicates that secular culture is leading Christians away from God's truth, creating a crisis within the church. Barna concludes,

> It's one thing for Americans to be confused on the finer points or even hotly debated elements of theology. But for Americans to misunderstand or to flat out reject the Bible as a foundational source of truth and moral guidance, to reject salvation by grace alone, and to reject core doctrines of the Christian faith points to a major crisis in our society.[5]

THE RATIONALE FOR RECLAIMING BIBLICAL LEADERSHIP

In their article, Watson and Scalen highlight how the church growth movement has led many churches to adopt cultural methods, essentially "reaching the culture by becoming the culture."[6] This approach has blurred the line between biblical leadership and secular leadership, replacing discipleship with marketing strategies and kingdom principles with corporate models. In *The Present Future: Six Tough Questions for the Church*, Reggie McNeal addresses this issue, noting,

> Church growth played to the dark side of some church leaders. The abuse of CEO privilege and position in Wall Street scandals has its counterpart in the church. The money and power that gravitate to leaders of large organizations

can place extra pressures on already-cracked character foundations. Under the all-growth-is-good mantra, some unscrupulous and spiritually suspect methodologies have been employed to 'get the numbers up.'[7]

McNeal highlights how the pursuit of growth at any cost can drive leaders to adopt ethically questionable strategies that undermine the spiritual integrity of their ministry. Instead of prioritizing faithfulness to biblical principles, many have fallen into the trap of seeking numerical success, often leading to moral and ethical compromises. The relentless drive for growth has fueled the emergence of a "celebrity-status church culture," cultivating unhealthy competition and unattainable standards within the church.[8]

The church growth movement's emphasis on methodologies and success has only intensified this problem, shifting the focus from spiritual depth to outward metrics. The effects of this unhealthy climate are evident in the leadership of the twenty-first-century American evangelical church, where a fixation on celebrity, status, wealth, and numerical success has contributed to the downfall of several prominent leaders.

Michael Youssef, senior pastor of the Church of the Apostles, emphasizes that many celebrity pastors struggle to maintain integrity under the pressures of fame. He suggests this issue arises because pastors often focus more on being celebrities and CEOs rather than serving and ministering as shepherds. Youssef further argues that this trend is a direct result of secularization.[9]

Gordon-Conwell Theological Seminary President and Missiology professor Scott Sunquist echoes this sentiment, warning of a "pandemic of narcissism" exacerbated by social media, which can transform minor self-esteem issues into full-blown narcissism. He asserts, "We have a pandemic of narcissism today. Social media feeds our small self-esteem appetite until it becomes a narcissistic monster. Most leaders fall into this trap." Sunquist argues that many leaders fail because they do not confront these issues and do not have strong, godly counsel guiding them toward holiness.[10] The pursuit of influence and notoriety has been disastrous for many prominent ministry leaders. A fixation on power and success, combined with a lack of character, often leads to ministerial failure. Although corporate leadership models can offer helpful insights to the church, they must never take precedence over the kingdom principles established in the Word of God.

In pursuit of success, many ministry leaders have increasingly turned to cultural trends and business models to define their leadership approach. This shift has led churches to measure success through performance metrics, consumer appeal, and numerical growth rather than spiritual depth. Management tools, marketing strategies, and statistics— though useful—have become dominant forces in shaping ministry decisions, particularly in the modern church growth movement. As a result, leaders often prioritize attracting and engaging audiences rather than cultivating deep discipleship, allowing secular values to overshadow kingdom principles.

When numbers and achievement take precedence over faithfulness to biblical truth, the church risks compromising its mission. Instead of fostering genuine spiritual transformation, leaders gravitate toward entertainment-driven approaches that cater to cultural expectations rather than scriptural convictions. When left unchecked, secular leadership methods replace kingdom principles and shift the focus from Christ-centered discipleship to audience retention. However, the values of the world directly oppose those of the kingdom of God. Ministry leaders must firmly reject any notion that God's principles are outdated or irrelevant. Instead of conforming to cultural pressures, leaders must remain steadfast—anchoring their leadership in the unchanging truth of God's Word.

In the article "Authentic Spiritual Leadership," Richard Mayhue, former Executive Vice President, Dean, and Professor of Pastoral Ministry and Theology at The Master's Seminary, highlights the crucial distinction needed in church leadership: the spiritual aspect must never be overlooked. He recounts asking a group of pastors to define "spiritual leadership," to which one replied, "Knowing where you are going and getting people to follow." When Mayhue pressed for a more thorough answer, it became clear that the pastor had focused exclusively on leadership, ignoring the spiritual dimension—a common mistake in the church today.

Mayhue argues that the church desperately needs strong spiritual leaders as defined by scripture, with Jesus as the ultimate model.[11] Jesus did not measure success by achievement or outcomes, but by the life He led. His leadership was marked by servanthood, humility, and obedience to the Father's will. As *the* kingdom leader, Jesus taught His disciples the kingdom way of leadership in the Sermon on the Mount, establishing non-negotiable principles for kingdom leadership. He emphasized that true leadership in the kingdom of God is not about power or status, but about serving others selflessly.

In *Redefining Leadership: Character-Driven Habits of Effective Leaders*, Joseph Stowell, former President of Moody Bible Institute and Cornerstone University, challenges church leaders by saying, "If the kingdom of Christ is not of this world, then it seems a great contradiction for kingdom of Christ leaders to be leading by advice and values that are of this world."[12] His statement underscores the fundamental distinction between worldly leadership and biblical leadership, emphasizing the need for leaders to reject secular influences in favor of Christ-centered principles. Therefore, those who follow Jesus must embrace and embody His leadership model to effectively lead others toward fulfilling God's mission. This ongoing commitment requires a daily dedication to surrendering personal ambition in favor of Christ's call to servanthood and faithfulness.

Many ministry leaders today fail to embody the biblical model of kingdom leadership that Jesus demonstrated. Instead, they have increasingly relied on secular strategies to achieve success in their churches. This approach often leads ministry leaders to depend on their personal charisma, marketing campaigns, and elevated production elements to drive attendance. While these strategies are not inherently wrong, they frequently replace biblically grounded teaching, leading to congregations that are numerically large but spiritually stagnant. True church growth is not measured in numbers alone but in transformed lives rooted in faithfulness to God's Word.

Some leaders contend that leadership is fundamentally about influence, asserting that its primary role is to guide others toward a shared purpose or vision. However, influence itself is neutral—its true impact depends on the direction in which it leads. For kingdom leaders, that direction must be clear: their ultimate responsibility is to guide people toward a life that follows Jesus. Their leadership should not be measured by personal charisma or outward success but by an unwavering commitment to leading others into deeper intimacy with Christ. True spiritual leadership requires a willingness to walk alongside others, discipling them with patience, humility, and love.

The Apostle Paul underscores this principle in 1 Corinthians 11:1 (NIV), "Follow my example, as I follow the example of Christ." Paul's leadership was not based on personal ambition or accolades but on his relentless pursuit of Christlikeness. Jesus called His disciples to follow Him, modeling what it means to live in complete obedience to the Father. He continues to call present-day ministry leaders to follow His example in leading the body of Christ with integrity and devotion.

Ministry leaders are called to be ambassadors for Christ, a role Paul reinforces in 2 Corinthians 5:20, "Therefore, we are ambassadors for Christ, God making his appeal through us." As ambassadors, ministry leaders are authorized representatives and messengers of Christ. They should embody His life and mission, reflecting His character and methodologies in their leadership. Their primary responsibility is not to build personal platforms or advance their own reputations, but to faithfully represent Christ and shepherd His people.

In *Lead: 12 Gospel Principles for Leadership in the Church*, Paul Tripp writes,

> It's time for us to confess that personal ambition often moves and shapes our leadership more than the gospel does. It's time to confess that as leaders we have given in to the temptation to be ambassadors of something other than our Lord. It's time to humbly admit that we cannot serve leadership idols and be ambassadors at the same time.[13]

This sobering statement calls church leaders to self-examination. If leadership becomes about personal recognition rather than Christ's glory, it has strayed from its true purpose.

The secularization of church leadership has presented a serious challenge, one that threatens to erode the spiritual foundation of ministry and transform the church into a reflection of worldly values. The focus on material success, celebrity status, and numerical growth has come at the expense of spiritual transformation. When churches place greater emphasis on entertainment and consumer-driven experiences, they risk losing sight of their ultimate purpose—to glorify God and make disciples.

The solution to this leadership dilemma lies in reclaiming the principles of the kingdom of God. Pastors and ministry leaders must resist the temptation to measure success by the world's standards and instead re-anchor their leadership in the teachings of scripture. This shift requires renewed commitment to prayer, dependence on the Holy Spirit, and a willingness to lead with humility and obedience. True kingdom leadership is not about building an empire but about shepherding God's people with love and integrity.

Church leaders are called to embody Christ-like leadership by remaining faithful to God's mission, nurturing deep spiritual growth, and shepherding their congregations with humility, integrity, and a servant's heart. This commitment requires an intentional shift—prioritizing discipleship over attendance numbers, genuine transformation over superficial engagement, and uncompromising biblical truth over fleeting cultural trends.

As ambassadors for Christ, pastors and ministry leaders must reject the allure of worldly success and recommit themselves to leading in alignment with the values of the kingdom of God. By doing so, they will not only strengthen their churches but also restore the church's transformative power in a world increasingly shaped by secular ideals. The call to biblical leadership is not simply an option; it is an urgent mandate. The church's effectiveness in fulfilling its mission hinges on leaders who are willing to forsake personal ambition, embrace the way of Christ, and lead with unwavering faithfulness to God's Word.

Chapter Two

LEADERSHIP AND POWER

Navigating Influence
with Biblical Integrity

THE INTERSECTION OF POWER AND BIBLICAL LEADERSHIP

IN THE RAPIDLY CHANGING CULTURE OF the modern church, the desire for influence and relevance has often overshadowed the foundational call for humility and service. As church leaders grapple with the pressures of success and growth, the challenge of wielding power with biblical integrity has become more pressing than ever. Pastors and ministry leaders frequently turn to leadership resources to improve their leadership abilities and address challenges within their churches and organizations. While many of these resources are developed out of practices and principles found in scripture, there is a tendency, as Benjamin Forrest, professor and administrative chair at Liberty University, and Chet Roden, Old Testament scholar and pastor, note, to "attempt to yoke biblical *principles* with unbiblical *practices, postures,* or *perspectives.*"[1] This reality underscores the critical need for a biblically-centered approach to leadership development, one that equips ministry leaders with Christ-centered practices and principles grounded in scripture. God has provided clear guidance through His Word and the example of His Son, offering a roadmap for ministry leaders in their leadership of self, others, and their churches and organizations. Thus, scripture must serve as the primary foundation for Christian leadership research and development.

In the realm of leadership, power plays a central role. Peter Northouse, Professor Emeritus of Communication and leadership consultant, defines power as "the capacity or potential to influence," highlighting its essential function in shaping beliefs, attitudes, and actions to achieve organizational goals. However, power has the potential to be a double-edged sword. When used ethically, it serves to inspire positive change and shared goals between leaders and followers. Conversely, when misused, power can become coercive, serving the leader's self-interests rather than the well-being of others.

Philosophers like Plato and Aristotle have long debated the ethical implications of power in leadership. Plato emphasized the importance of selecting leaders with a strong sense of justice, while Aristotle stressed the need for self-leadership to prevent corruption. Both recognized that power has the potential to magnify a leader's character traits, for better or worse. The "Bathsheba Syndrome," drawn from the biblical story of King David, illustrates how power can lead to moral failure, especially in leaders who are otherwise successful.

The challenge of power in leadership remains as relevant today as it was in ancient times. Leaders must be vigilant in developing virtues such as judgment, courage, justice, and humility to safeguard against the corrupting influence of power. As scholars Rachel Sturm and Lucas Monzani suggest, virtuous leaders are best equipped to wield power for the greater good, underscoring the need for strong character in leadership.

This chapter explores the intricate dynamics of power in leadership, highlighting both its potential for positive influence and its capacity for corruption. By addressing the ethical challenges associated with power, it offers pastors and ministry leaders a comprehensive framework for using power responsibly, rooted in the virtues and character traits that reflect Christ-centered leadership.

THE ROLE OF POWER IN LEADERSHIP

Power is inherently tied to leadership because of its integral role in the process of influence. Peter Northouse notes, "Power is the capacity or potential to influence. People have power when they have the ability to affect others' beliefs, attitudes, and courses of action."[2] In essence, power is the tool leaders use to initiate change within individuals to achieve organizational goals. However, the way power is wielded can either build or destroy.

Leaders who use power for personal gain or to control others exhibit what is often termed the "dark side" of leadership, where power becomes coercive—characterized by force, manipulation, and threats. This kind of power typically serves the leader's interests rather than benefiting followers or the organization as a whole. In contrast, leadership scholar James Burns offers a more positive perspective, emphasizing that power in leadership should be about achieving the shared goals of both leaders and followers.[3]

Power is frequently defined as "the potential ability of one person to influence others to carry out orders"[4] or to compel others "to do something they otherwise would not have done."[5] These definitions highlight power's ability to fulfill the leader's goals or reach their desired outcomes. Within organizations, power generally falls into two categories: positional and personal. Positional power comes from holding a specific office or rank, giving the leader influence derived from their status. Personal power, on the other hand, is rooted in the leader's likability and expertise. When leaders act in ways that matter to their followers, they gain power—whether through their position or personal attributes.

However, power is a double-edged sword. While it can be used to influence followers positively and achieve organizational goals, it is also susceptible to misuse in toxic and destructive ways. Abusive leadership, for instance, occurs when power is used for personal gain rather than the organization's benefit. Some individuals seek leadership roles primarily to gain access to power, driven by a desire to control others rather than to serve.

The more followers a leader has, the greater their power, and with that power comes the ability to influence—whether through pressure, flattery, or rational persuasion.

THE ETHICAL CHALLENGES OF POWER

The ethical use of power has long been a subject of philosophical debate. Plato and Aristotle, for instance, were deeply concerned with the moral implications of power in leadership. Plato emphasized the importance of character in selecting leaders, arguing that only those with a highly developed sense of justice should wield power. He believed leaders must be carefully chosen and held accountable to ensure they do not use power for self-serving purposes. Aristotle agreed with Plato on the importance of selecting virtuous leaders but placed greater emphasis on self-leadership, arguing that leaders must master their passions to prevent power from corrupting them. For Aristotle, the ability to lead oneself was the most critical quality of a good leader.

The discussion of power in leadership should focus not only on defining power but also on understanding the qualities that make for exemplary leadership. A critical aspect of this development involves understanding the role of power in leadership. Plato and Aristotle recognized that the temptations of power are among the greatest challenges leaders face. Joanne Ciulla, director of the Institute for Ethical Leadership, notes, "The power that leaders have to do things also entails the power to hide what they do. Power carries with it a temptation to do evil and an obligation to do good."[6]

Understanding power is just the beginning; applying it with integrity is the challenge every leader must face. The story of King David and Bathsheba serves as a vivid reminder that even the most successful leaders are vulnerable to the corrupting influence of power. David, a man after God's own heart, allowed his authority to cloud his judgment, leading to devastating moral failure. His story cautions today's leaders to remain vigilant and grounded in humility, no matter how much influence they wield. The Bathsheba Syndrome—a term coined from the biblical account of King David—illustrates the dangers of pride and moral weakness in leadership. This syndrome describes leaders who, when faced with power and success, struggle to respond in an ethical manner. David's personal immorality and abuse of power caused significant harm to his followers, serving as a cautionary tale about the potential for leaders to misuse their power and privilege. Often, leaders who become successful are at greater risk of falling into this syndrome, making it difficult to predict who might be affected by such a shift in character. Therefore, the ethical challenges associated with power must be a central consideration in the development of leaders.

The power that comes with leadership often brings a strong temptation for leaders to use their influence for self-serving purposes. Leaders driven by a desire for power and control are more likely to ignore social norms and less likely to embrace the challenges and sacrifices that come with ethical leadership. This tendency reveals that a leader's true character is often exposed when they are granted power. Plato and Aristotle's warnings about the corrupting nature of power remain relevant today; their insights suggest that great care must be taken in selecting leaders because power has the tendency to amplify a person's character traits. When power is misused, it can drive leaders to prioritize personal gain over the welfare of others, resulting in corrupt leadership. Such corruption not only violates social norms but also harms the greater good of society. To guard against the corrosive effects of power, leaders must cultivate both the skill to lead others effectively and the self-discipline to govern their own actions.

CULTIVATING VIRTUOUS LEADERSHIP

Aristotle argued that power is not inherently bad but becomes corrupt when exercised by those with weak or immoral character. He believed that virtuous character is developed through habitual virtuous behavior and that good leadership is rooted in good character. Therefore, effective leadership is grounded in strong character, which serves as a safeguard against the corrupting influence of power.

To counteract the corrupting influence of power, leaders must cultivate virtues such as judgment, courage, humanity, justice, temperance, transcendence, accountability, drive, collaboration, humility, and integrity. Among these, judgment is particularly crucial, as it enables leaders to responsibly manage the challenges and temptations associated with power.

Rachel Sturm and Lucas Monzani echo the sentiments of Plato and Aristotle, concluding that virtuous leaders are best suited to handle power because they will use it for the greater good. In light of the increasing instances of power abuse in leadership, they argue that the real crisis we face today is not merely one of power and corruption but of a lack of leader character.[7]

A CHRIST-CENTERED APPROACH TO POWER

In examining the role of power in leadership, it becomes clear that the influence leaders employ is both a powerful tool for positive change and a potential source of corruption. The ethical use of power, grounded in biblical principles, requires strong moral character in leadership. When leaders are driven by self-interest or unchecked ambition, they risk falling into the "dark side" of leadership, where power is exploited to manipulate or control others for personal gain.

For ministry leaders, the critical challenge is aligning their leadership with Christ's example, using their influence to serve others and promote God's kingdom. A Christ-centered approach to power is crucial, urging leaders to anchor their authority in biblical principles. By doing so, they can wield their influence with integrity and purpose, ultimately serving as powerful examples of Christ-like leadership for those they lead.

THE RESPONSIBILITY OF POWER

The responsibility of power in leadership demands a careful balance of authority, integrity, and service. Ministry leaders must intentionally align their influence with the example set by Christ, ensuring that their leadership is grounded in biblical principles rather than personal ambition. Power, when used with wisdom and humility, can become a transformative force that fosters growth, unity, and spiritual maturity within the church and beyond. However, without vigilance and a commitment to character, it can easily lead to corruption and harm. Leaders are called to reflect on their use of power, cultivating virtues that mirror Christ-like leadership—serving others, prioritizing their well-being, and using their influence to advance God's kingdom with integrity. Leadership in the kingdom is not about personal gain, but about faithfully guiding others toward a deeper relationship with Christ. It is through this lens that power must be exercised responsibly, with an unwavering focus on the greater good.

Chapter Three

THE KINGDOM OF GOD

A Central
Biblical Theme

THE KINGDOM OF GOD AS THE HEART OF SCRIPTURE

THE KINGDOM of God is more than just a theological idea; it is the central, unifying theme that runs throughout scripture, woven from the Old Testament's declaration of God's sovereign rule over Israel and the world to the New Testament's detailed exploration of this concept, particularly in the teachings of Jesus. This kingdom is not merely a realm; it represents God's authority, power, and divine plan to redeem humanity.

In this chapter, the multifaceted nature of the kingdom of God will be explored—its present reality and future fulfillment, its mysteries revealed through Christ, and the profound decision it demands from every individual. The kingdom of God is not merely a realm but the essence of God's rule and reign, requiring total submission, offering eternal life, and demanding a response that shapes one's eternal destiny.

DEFINING THE KINGDOM OF GOD

The concept of the kingdom of God begins in the Old Testament, where God's kingship is established over Israel and all the earth. This theme is further developed in the New Testament, particularly in the Synoptic Gospels of Matthew, Mark, and Luke. The terms "kingdom of God" and "kingdom of heaven" are often used interchangeably in scripture, as noted by scholars J.D. Douglas and Merrill C. Tenney.[1] The biblical concept of "kingdom" refers to the rank, authority, and sovereignty exercised by a king, with the Old Testament using the Hebrew word *malkuth* and the New Testament employing the Greek term *basileia*.[2] According to Douglas and Tenney, the kingdom of God represents "his sovereign activity as King in saving sinners and overcoming evil."[3] God, as the sovereign King, has absolute authority over His kingdom, which includes both the heavens and the earth—His realm.

The kingdom of God signifies God's reign, rule, and sovereignty over all things. George Eldon Ladd, professor and evangelical scholar, succinctly states, "God's Kingdom is His power."[4] The Psalms often speak of God's kingdom and power, declaring, "They shall speak of the glory of your kingdom and tell of your power" (Psalm 145:11) and "Your kingdom is an everlasting kingdom, and your dominion endures throughout all generations" (Psalm 145:13). These verses underscore the eternal nature of God's rule, reinforcing the theme of God's sovereignty woven throughout scripture.

THE REALMS OF THE KINGDOM OF GOD

God's sovereign rule extends across different realms and can be experienced both in the present and the future to varying degrees. Throughout redemptive history, God's reign has been revealed at various stages, with each era offering a glimpse of His kingdom. While heaven represents the age to come—a time when humanity will fully experience the complete blessings of God in their perfection—His kingdom can also be partially experienced here and now. The Second Coming of Christ, known as the *parousia*, will mark the end of the present age and usher in the fullness of God's reign in the age to come.

This current age, however, stands in stark contrast to the age to come. The present world is characterized by evil, sin, unrighteousness, and rebellion against God. The Apostle Paul describes the destructive behaviors of this age in Galatians 5:19-21:

> Now the works of the flesh are evident: sexual immorality, impurity, sensuality, idolatry, sorcery, enmity, strife, jealousy, fits of anger, rivalries, dissensions, divisions, envy, drunkenness, orgies, and things like these. I warn, as I warned you before, that those who do such things will not inherit the kingdom of God.

Through this warning, Paul underscores the serious consequences for those who engage in these actions, stressing that they will not inherit the kingdom of God. The environment of the present age is hostile to the gospel, as Satan has been granted limited power and authority to influence humanity. Paul explains in 2 Corinthians 4:4 that "the god of this world has blinded the minds of the unbelievers, to keep them from seeing the light of the gospel of the glory of Christ, who is the image of God." As a result, the truth of the kingdom remains hidden from those who reject the scriptures, blinded by Satan's deception. Satan actively works to obstruct the spread of the kingdom's message, steering this age toward deeper rebellion against God. For believers, this opposition brings inevitable trials, as they encounter intense hostility in their commitment to faithfulness.

Despite the affliction and hostility that believers may face in this age, the powers of the coming age have already begun to infiltrate the present. Christ's death and resurrection have made it possible for believers to be empowered and delivered from the evil that dominates this world. As Paul writes in Galatians 1:4, Christ "gave himself for our sins to deliver us from the present evil age, according to the will of our God and Father." Through this redemptive act, believers can endure and overcome the challenges of this age, holding onto the hope of the age to come.

In contrast to the present, the age to come will be characterized by eternal life, salvation, and the perfect fullness of God's kingdom. To enter this future kingdom, one must be born again—a truth that Jesus emphasized in His conversation with Nicodemus in John 3:3-5:

> Jesus answered him, "Truly, truly, I say to you, unless one is born again he cannot see the kingdom of God." Nicodemus said to him, "How can a man be born when he is old? Can he enter a second time into his mother's womb and be born?" Jesus answered, "Truly, truly, I say to you, unless one is born of water and the Spirit, he cannot enter the kingdom of God."

Jesus makes it clear that being born again is essential to seeing and entering the kingdom of God. This new birth requires more than merely following the law or relying on privileged positions; it demands a personal relationship with Jesus and a complete spiritual renewal.

The kingdom of heaven, marked by righteousness, will be fully realized after the Second Coming of Christ. At that time, the enemy will be utterly defeated, and there will be no more evil, wickedness, or sin. Only Christ has the power to bring about this new age, and His return will inaugurate the final and perfect reign of God's kingdom.

THE MYSTERY OF THE KINGDOM OF GOD

The kingdom of God is a mystery, a hidden truth that is revealed only to those who are born again. Jesus illustrated this concept when He explained to His disciples why He spoke in parables: "To you it has been given to know the secrets of the kingdom of heaven, but to them it has not been given" (Matthew 13:11). In his work, *The Kingdom of God*, Martyn Lloyd-Jones identifies Christ Himself as the mystery of the kingdom because it is through Him that the kingdom is revealed.[5] The Apostle Paul echoes this sentiment in 1 Timothy 3:16, where he describes the mystery of godliness as Christ, "manifested in the flesh, vindicated by the Spirit, seen by angels, proclaimed among nations, believed on in the world, taken up in glory."

The greatest mystery of the kingdom of God lies in God's plan to save humanity through Christ's sacrificial death on the cross. This act of redemption is offered to all, but each individual must choose to accept it. Jesus emphasized the difficulty of this choice in Matthew 7:14, where He stated, "For the gate is narrow and the way is hard that leads to life, and those who find it are few." Salvation requires absolute submission to God and acceptance of His way, which is only possible through Christ. As Jesus declared in John 14:6, "I am the way, and the truth, and the life. No one comes to the Father except through me." Preaching plays a crucial role in this process, as it plants the Word of God in the hearts of the hearers, and the Holy Spirit works to bring about a profound transformation.

The final mystery awaiting God's people is future glory—Christ's return, which will destroy all tribulation and usher in a new kingdom. The Apostle Peter spoke of this future in 2 Peter 3:13, describing "new heavens and a new earth in which righteousness dwells." This new kingdom will be free from sin, and God's people will be made righteous by their faith in Christ. The tragedy within the mystery of the kingdom lies in the reality that not everyone will receive it—God does not impose the kingdom upon anyone; instead, each individual must actively seek salvation and its abundant blessings. The parable of the sower in Matthew 13 captures this dynamic vividly: some will embrace the gospel seed, others will reject it, and still others will fail to understand, deceived by Satan's influence. The kingdom is a costly gift, requiring each person to choose to surrender their will and heart to God in order to inherit His kingdom.

THE KINGDOM DEMANDS A DECISION

The most critical decision any person will ever make is whether to enter the kingdom of God. God's Word requires a response; every individual who hears it must choose either to accept or reject it—a decision regarding the kingdom cannot remain neutral. As Hebrews 12:25 warns, "See that you do not refuse him who is speaking." God speaks through scripture and has provided all the resources necessary to live an abundant life through Christ. However, entering His kingdom requires more than mere acknowledgment—it demands heeding His warnings, receiving Christ, and living according to His truths. God sent His only Son into the world to redeem humanity from an eternity of evil and darkness.

In the Gospel of Matthew, Jesus urged His disciples to seek the kingdom first, fully aware of the profound significance of this choice. He knew that, one day, every person would stand before God in judgment, accountable for whether they embraced or disregarded His words.

Entrance into God's kingdom requires restoration through new birth—a complete transformation that necessitates the death of one's former way of life. This rebirth transcends mere behavior modification; it calls for a life completely surrendered to God, dedicated entirely to His glory. The reborn life centers on loving God with all one's heart, mind, soul, and strength.

Martyn Lloyd-Jones describes the kingdom of God as "entering into the spiritual realm, into fellowship with the almighty and the everlasting God. It means being a citizen of God's kingdom; it means walking with him." He continues, "It is the realm of light and glory; and before I can enter it I must have something in me that corresponds to that."[6] Thus, regeneration is necessary because no one can enter the kingdom of God in their natural state. The kingdom is the dwelling place of God, and communion with Him requires that each person be born again.

Belief in Jesus as God incarnate—God in the flesh, who brings personal redemption—is fundamental to receiving the kingdom of God. This salvation demands obedience to His teachings and an understanding of one's inherent sinful nature. As Jesus taught in Matthew 16:24-26:

Then Jesus told his disciples, "If anyone would come after me, let him deny himself and take up his cross and follow me. For whoever would save his life will lose it, but whoever loses his life for my sake will find it. For what will it profit a man if he gains the whole world and forfeits his soul? Or what shall a man give in return for his soul?"

Following Him requires self-denial and a willingness to lose one's life for His sake to gain eternal life in the kingdom. The decision to follow Christ and enter His kingdom is not one of mere convenience or temporary change; it is a profound, life-altering choice that determines one's eternal destiny.

THE KINGDOM OF GOD AS A CALL TO FAITHFULNESS AND TRANSFORMATION

The kingdom of God stands as the central theme of scripture, encapsulating God's sovereign rule, His plan for redemption, and the call for humanity to enter into His divine reign. The kingdom is not merely a future hope but a present reality that requires a response from every individual. It demands submission, transformation, and faithfulness to God's will as revealed through Christ.

Understanding the nature of God's kingdom, both its present and future dimensions, compels believers to live with the awareness that their decisions and actions have eternal significance. Entering this kingdom requires more than intellectual acknowledgment—it involves a life-changing commitment to follow Christ and align one's heart with God's purposes. The kingdom calls for a response, urging believers to turn from sin, embrace the new birth, and live as citizens of a spiritual realm where righteousness, peace, and joy in the Holy Spirit reign supreme.

In the end, the kingdom of God is not only a theological concept but the ultimate invitation to a life transformed by Christ's power and presence. It is a kingdom that offers hope, renewal, and eternal life to those who respond in faith and obedience. The challenge and the privilege lie in the decision to enter this kingdom and live fully under God's righteous reign.

Chapter Four

JESUS AND THE KINGDOM OF GOD

JESUS: THE EMBODIMENT AND REVELATION OF THE KINGDOM

IN THE LIFE and ministry of Jesus, the kingdom of God was not merely a topic of discussion—it was the very essence of His mission. Jesus embodied the kingdom, making it a living, breathing reality that could be seen, touched, and experienced by those around Him. This chapter explores how Jesus not only taught about the kingdom but lived it, revealing through His actions what it truly means to be under God's sovereign rule.

From His earliest teachings to His final moments on earth, Jesus consistently pointed to the kingdom as the central focus of His life and work. He did not simply explain the kingdom; He demonstrated it in every interaction, every miracle, and every word. The kingdom was inseparable from Jesus Himself, as He was both its messenger and its manifestation.

As this chapter unfolds, the profound connection between Jesus and the kingdom of God will be examined,
highlighting how He modeled kingdom living and how His
followers are called to continue His mission. Through Jesus,
the kingdom of God is revealed in its fullness, inviting all
who follow Him to live under God's reign and to bring the
light of the kingdom into every aspect of their lives.

JESUS: THE KINGDOM MADE FLESH

In Jesus, the embodiment of the kingdom of God is revealed. The kingdom wasn't just a topic Jesus taught about;
it was the very heart of His mission and the core of His
life's work. Every word He spoke and every action He took
was infused with the purpose of revealing the kingdom to
those around Him.

The early Christian theologian Origen of Alexandria
captured this profound truth when he used the term "au-
tobasileia" to describe Jesus, meaning "the kingdom in person." In his commentary on Matthew 18, Origen wrote,

> If it be likened to such a king, and one who had
> done such things, who must we say that it is but
> the Son of God? For He is the King of the heavens,
> and as He is absolute Wisdom and absolute Righ-
> teousness and absolute Truth, is He not so also
> absolute Kingdom?[1]

In Jesus, the kingdom of God was not just a concept; it was a living, breathing reality. To know Jesus is to know the kingdom; to understand the kingdom is to understand Jesus. The two are inseparable. Theologian Jürgen Moltmann emphasized this connection, stating,

> If, therefore, one wants to learn what the mysterious 'Kingdom of God' actually is, then one must look to Jesus. And if one wants to understand who Jesus actually is, then one must experience the Kingdom of God.[2]

Jesus never provided a definition of the kingdom of God to His followers. Instead, He demonstrated it through His life. Every interaction, every teaching, every miracle was a glimpse into the kingdom. Through His actions, Jesus allowed His followers to experience the kingdom firsthand, showing them what it means to live under God's reign. The Apostle John, in his first letter, reflected on this deeply meaningful reality, writing,

> That which was from the beginning, which we have heard, which we have seen with our eyes, which we looked upon and have touched with our hands, concerning the word of life—the life was made manifest, and we have seen it, and testify to it and proclaim to you the eternal life, which was with the Father and

was made manifest to us—that which we have seen and heard we proclaim also to you (1 John 1:1-3).

The disciples were eyewitnesses to the kingdom through Jesus. They didn't just hear about it; they saw it, touched it, and lived it. Their experiences with Jesus were so transformative that they dedicated their lives to sharing this kingdom life with others. They desired everyone to experience the kingdom as they had, to live in the reality of God's reign as they had seen it embodied in Jesus.

Jesus consistently urged His followers to seek the kingdom of God above all else. He called them not just to believe in the kingdom, but to fully embrace it—living it out as their highest priority. This call remains for all believers today. Jesus invites each person to partner with Him in His kingdom, carrying forward the mission of bringing God's reign into every area of life and transforming the world around them. The kingdom was Jesus' greatest concern, and it should likewise be the focus for all who follow Him. In every age, the kingdom of God continues to be the central focus for His followers, guiding how they live, serve, and lead.

THE KINGDOM REVEALED: JESUS' MISSION AND MESSAGE

When Jesus began His public ministry, He entered Galilee with a bold proclamation: the gospel of the kingdom of God had arrived. In Mark 1:14-15, it is written, "Jesus came into Galilee, proclaiming the gospel of God, and saying, 'The time is fulfilled, and the kingdom of God is at hand; repent and believe in the gospel.'" This announcement was the cornerstone of Jesus' mission, an authoritative declaration that God's plan for the world was unfolding.

From the beginning, God's purpose was to deliver humanity from sin and shame, a plan set in motion long before time began. Paul writes in 1 Corinthians 2:7, "But we impart a secret and hidden wisdom of God, which God decreed before the ages for our glory." The prophets and teachers of the Old Testament hinted at this divine plan, but its fulfillment was realized in the life and ministry of Jesus. When Jesus declared, "the time is fulfilled," He was revealing that the long-awaited kingdom of God had arrived in Him.

In His synagogue sermon in Nazareth, Jesus revealed Himself as the embodiment of the gospel, declaring that the kingdom of God had arrived in His very person. He proclaimed,

The Spirit of the Lord is upon me, because he has anointed me to proclaim good news to the poor. He has sent me to proclaim liberty to the captives and recovering of sight to the blind, to set at liberty those who are oppressed, to proclaim the year of the Lord's favor (Luke 4:18-19).

Jesus' proclamation marks the direct fulfillment of Isaiah 61:1-2, bringing the long-awaited promises of the Old Testament to fruition. His ministry, defined by preaching the good news to the needy and performing mighty works, confirms Him as the appointed Messiah, anointed by the Spirit to bring salvation to the world. The purpose of the gospel, then, is to bring freedom and healing to all who will receive it. In Jesus, the kingdom of God arrives, imparting God's reign and rule, and with it comes righteousness, peace, blessings, favor, hope, and triumph over evil for all who place their faith in Him. As heirs to this kingdom, God's people receive the spiritual blessings that flow from their new life in Christ. Yet, there remains only one path into the kingdom—through Christ's sacrificial death on the cross. His immense love for humanity led Him to the crucifixion, creating a way through the narrow gate that invites all who seek Him to enter.

The mission and ministry of Jesus were entirely rooted in the kingdom of God, which was His foremost concern and guiding purpose. His teachings are intended to lead people into the kingdom, showing them the way to enter and live within it. In Matthew 5:20, Jesus warned, "For I tell you, unless your righteousness exceeds that of the scribes and the Pharisees, you will never enter the kingdom of heaven." And in Matthew 7:21, He said, "Not everyone who says to me, 'Lord, Lord,' will enter the kingdom of heaven, but the one who does the will of my Father who is in heaven." Jesus' mighty works, such as casting out demons, affirmed the presence of the kingdom, as He stated in Matthew 12:28, "But if it is by the Spirit of God that I cast out demons, then the kingdom of God has come upon you."

Jesus used parables to reveal the mysteries of the kingdom to His disciples, saying, "To you it has been given to know the secrets of the kingdom of heaven, but to them it has not been given" (Matthew 13:11). He taught them to pray for the kingdom, "Your kingdom come, your will be done, on earth as it is in heaven" (Matthew 6:10). On the night before His death, Jesus invited His disciples to share in the fellowship and blessings of the kingdom with Him, saying, "You are those who have stayed with me in my trials, and I assign to you, as my Father assigned to me, a kingdom, that you may eat and drink at my table in my kingdom and sit on thrones judging the twelve tribes of Israel" (Luke 22:28-30).

Jesus ultimately assures His followers that He will return in glory to deliver the full inheritance of the kingdom to God's people. In Matthew 25:31-34, Jesus describes the final judgment, stating,

> When the Son of Man comes in his glory, and all the angels with him, then he will sit on his glorious throne. Before him will be gathered all the nations, and he will separate people one from another as a shepherd separates the sheep from the goats. And he will place the sheep on his right, but the goats on the left. Then the King will say to those on his right, "Come, you who are blessed by my Father, inherit the kingdom prepared for you from the foundation of the world."

Here, Jesus emphasizes the sharp division between the righteous and unrighteous, highlighting the eternal inheritance awaiting those who are faithful.

For Jesus, the kingdom of God was the ultimate priority. He urged His followers to seek it above all else, instructing them in Matthew 6:33, "But seek first the kingdom of God and his righteousness, and all these things will be added to you." Jesus emphasized that the kingdom must be the driving force in the lives of His followers. They are called to live in a way that is distinctly different from those who do not know Him, not pursuing temporary things but instead focusing on the eternal. Scholars Carson, Wessell, and Liefeld explain,

> To seek first the kingdom is to desire above all to enter into, submit to, and participate in spreading the news of the saving reign of God, the messianic kingdom already inaugurated by Jesus, and to live so as to store up treasures in heaven in the prospect of the kingdom's consummation.[3]

In every aspect of His life and ministry, Jesus demonstrated that the kingdom of God was central. His teachings, miracles, and promises all pointed to the reality of God's reign breaking into the world through Him, calling His followers to live under that reign with complete devotion.

JESUS: THE MODEL OF KINGDOM LIVING

Jesus initiated His earthly ministry by carefully selecting His disciples and inviting them to follow Him closely. From the very beginning, Jesus wasn't merely a teacher; He was a mentor, a living example of what it meant to embody the kingdom of God. The kingdom wasn't just a theme in His teachings; it was the very essence of His life. Every word He spoke, every action He took, was a reflection of the kingdom's values and principles.

When Jesus called His disciples, He wasn't simply gathering students—He was inviting them into a way of life. He modeled for them how to live as heirs of the kingdom, demonstrating not only what they were to believe but how they were to act, think, and serve. The kingdom of God was the cornerstone of His mission, shaping every aspect of His actions and teachings. Pastor and evangelist F. B. Meyer insightfully remarked,

> Our Lord for thirty years was content to live an absolutely holy life, as the Lamb of God without blemish and without spot; and His supreme work in the world was not only to give His life as a ransom, but to live His life that He might leave us an example that we should follow in His steps.[4]

Similarly, the Apostle Peter, in his letter, urged believers to walk in the footsteps of Jesus, who not only suffered but also embodied the ultimate standard of holy living: "For to this you have been called, because Christ also suffered for you, leaving you an example, so that you might follow in his steps" (1 Peter 2:21).

From a young age, Jesus demonstrated a profound awareness of His mission. Luke 2:49 portrays Jesus as a boy already deeply focused on His Father's work. When His parents found Him in the temple, He explained, "Did you not know that I must be in my Father's house?" Even then, His life was directed toward fulfilling God's will. Later, in His ministry, Jesus made it clear that His primary goal was to glorify the Father. In John 17:4, He prays, "I glorified you on earth, having accomplished the work that you gave me to do." For Jesus, living a holy life meant living to glorify God in everything, a theme He stressed to His disciples during the Sermon on the Mount. "Let your light shine before others," He urged, "so that they may see your good works and give glory to your Father who is in heaven" (Matthew 5:16). Jesus' life was driven by this singular purpose, which He embodied fully and urged His disciples to embrace and follow wholeheartedly.

Prayer was another cornerstone of Jesus' life, and He taught its importance by example. Jesus didn't merely instruct His disciples to pray—He demonstrated it through His own actions. His life was saturated with prayer, and His disciples, moved by His example, asked Him to teach them how to pray. This moment is captured in Luke 11:2-4, where Jesus provides a model for prayer, guiding them with these words, "When you pray, say: Father, hallowed be Your name. Your kingdom come. Give us each day our daily bread, and forgive us our sins, for we ourselves forgive everyone who is indebted to us. And lead us not into temptation." Jesus' prayer life was not just a private matter; it was a powerful teaching tool, a way to connect His disciples with the Father and align them with the kingdom's purposes.

Jesus earned the trust of His followers by living a life that exemplified true discipleship. He consistently directed their focus toward the kingdom, guiding them with His teachings, mentorship, and challenges. His leadership was characterized by humility and servanthood. Jesus demonstrated unwavering courage and boldness, standing firmly for kingdom values and principles. His ultimate mission was to fulfill the Father's will, even to the point of death on a cross, embodying love, sacrifice, and forgiveness. In doing so, He established a model for every disciple striving to walk in His footsteps.

Jesus' example was not limited to the disciples of His time—it applies to every follower of Christ. He is the model for how believers are to live, serve, and lead within the kingdom of God. His life perfectly reflected kingdom values, and He calls all His followers to walk in His footsteps, living out those same values in their own lives. By embracing this calling, they advance the mission of the kingdom, bringing its light into the world just as Jesus Himself did.

JESUS AND THE KINGDOM OF GOD—A CALL TO LIVE AND LEAD UNDER HIS REIGN

In examining the life and ministry of Jesus, it becomes clear that the kingdom of God is not an abstract idea but a tangible reality, brought to life in every word, action, and miracle of Christ. Jesus not only proclaimed the kingdom but embodied it, demonstrating what it means to live fully under God's sovereign rule. His mission was to reveal this kingdom to the world, inviting all who would follow Him to experience the transformative power of God's reign.

This chapter has highlighted the inseparable connection between Jesus and the kingdom of God, emphasizing that to understand one is to know the other. Jesus' life was a living model of kingdom living, offering a clear example for His disciples—and all future believers—to follow. Through His teachings, prayer, and sacrificial love, Jesus provided a roadmap for how believers are to live as citizens of God's kingdom.

For those who follow Christ today, the call is the same: to seek the kingdom above all else, to reflect its values in their daily lives, and to carry forward Jesus' mission of bringing the kingdom's light into the world. The kingdom of God, revealed in Jesus, continues to demand a response from each believer—a response of faith, submission, and action as they strive to live under God's reign and lead others toward His eternal kingdom.

Chapter Five

CHARACTERISTICS OF THE KINGDOM OF GOD

UNVEILING THE HEART OF THE KINGDOM THROUGH JESUS

THIS CHAPTER DELVES into the deep connection between Jesus and the kingdom of God, showing how His life, teachings, and mission revealed the true nature of the kingdom. Jesus didn't just speak about the kingdom; He personified it, bringing the abstract idea of God's reign to life in a way that was tangible and accessible to all. Through His intimate relationship with the Father, His steadfast focus on the kingdom, His emphasis on true righteousness, and His demonstration of divine power, Jesus provided a living example of what it means to live under God's rule.

To understand this kingdom, one must first examine Jesus' deep communion with the Father, which served as the foundation for His ministry. From an early age, Jesus displayed a clear understanding of His mission, consistently prioritizing His Father's will above all else. This relationship was not only one of obedience but also of deep, personal communion, exemplified by Jesus' life of prayer and solitude.

The focus then turns to how Jesus placed the kingdom of God at the very heart of His ministry, urging His followers to seek it above all other pursuits. The kingdom was not simply a future promise but a present reality, introduced through Jesus' teachings, parables, and miraculous works. He called for a righteousness that went beyond superficial adherence to the law—a righteousness born from a deeply transformed heart, fully aligned with God's will.

Another essential aspect of the kingdom is its power, vividly demonstrated by Jesus. His authority permeated every facet of His ministry, from healing the sick to casting out demons. This power was not merely a display of divine strength; it served as a definitive sign that the kingdom of God had broken into the world, offering freedom and transformation to all willing to enter.

The chapter also considers the early church's challenges in understanding and living out the principles of the kingdom. Despite these difficulties, the apostles remained dedicated to guiding the fledgling communities back to the core teachings of Jesus, emphasizing the importance of aligning their lives with kingdom values.

In essence, Jesus didn't just teach about the kingdom of God; He lived it, making it the central theme of His life and ministry. His example calls believers to embody kingdom principles in every area of life, bringing God's reign into every aspect of their existence.

RELATIONSHIP WITH THE FATHER

From a young age, Jesus understood the importance of His relationship with the Father, a connection that would define His life and ministry. Even as a child, He made it clear to His parents that His ultimate purpose was to fulfill the will of His Father, saying, "Why did you seek Me? Did you not know that I must be about My Father's business?" (Luke 2:49, NKJV). This moment revealed Jesus' deep commitment to His divine mission, one that even His parents found challenging to fully grasp.

Throughout His ministry, Jesus modeled total dependence on the Father, consistently seeking solitude and prayer to align Himself with God's will. For example, before choosing His twelve disciples, He spent an entire night in prayer, highlighting the importance of divine guidance in each decision: "In these days he went out to the mountain to pray, and all night he continued in prayer to God. And when day came, he called his disciples and chose from them twelve, whom he named apostles" (Luke 6:12-13). This pattern of retreating for solitary prayer was a cornerstone of Jesus' life, a practice His disciples frequently observed as He sought communion with the Father both in the quiet of the morning and the stillness of the night. Jesus modeled a life of prayer, demonstrating to His followers the necessity of a deep, personal relationship with God.

Though fully divine and capable of acting independently, Jesus chose to humble Himself, relying entirely on the Father. He spoke only what the Father instructed, acted in accordance with the Father's will, and made it His mission to glorify God in all things. Jesus' life was a living testament to God's presence and power, and He called His followers to be lights in the world, reflecting the glory of the Father (Matthew 5:16). For Jesus, glorifying God wasn't just a goal—it was the very essence of His life.

The Apostle Paul, in his letter to the Ephesians, urged believers to be "imitators of God" (Ephesians 5:1). Imitation requires intimacy; to truly reflect God's character, one must cultivate a deep, personal relationship with Him. Paul elaborates in 2 Corinthians, stating, "And we all, with unveiled face, beholding the glory of the Lord, are being transformed into the same image from one degree of glory to another" (2 Corinthians 3:18). This transformation, achieved through worship, prayer, scripture study, and fellowship within the body of Christ, draws believers closer to God, enabling them to reflect His character.

Jesus fully understood the necessity of this relationship with the Father. His love for God was profound, and His desire to please Him was unwavering. This deep connection required significant time spent in prayer and solitude, and through these practices, Jesus was continually encouraged, empowered, and equipped for His mission. Jesus, who perfectly modeled this relationship with the Father, invites His followers to do the same—to seek the Father, to love Him deeply, and to live in a way that glorifies Him.

SEEKING THE KINGDOM

The kingdom of God was central to Jesus' mission and ministry, and He emphasized its significance by urging His followers to prioritize it above all else: "But seek first the kingdom of God and his righteousness, and all these things will be added to you" (Matthew 6:33). Jesus made clear that the kingdom of God should be the driving force in His people's lives, setting it above the pursuit of worldly, temporal things.

In His teachings, Jesus clearly outlined the path to entering God's kingdom, emphasizing the importance of righteousness and obedience to the Father's will. He warned in Matthew 5:20, "For I tell you, unless your righteousness exceeds that of the scribes and Pharisees, you will never enter the kingdom of heaven." Further underscoring this teaching, He stated in Matthew 7:21, "Not everyone who says to me, 'Lord, Lord,' will enter the kingdom of heaven, but the one who does the will of my Father who is in heaven." Through His miracles and mighty works, Jesus offered tangible demonstrations that the kingdom of God had truly arrived, declaring, "But if it is by the Spirit of God that I cast out demons, then the kingdom of God has come upon you" (Matthew 12:28).

Jesus often used parables to reveal the mysteries of the kingdom, providing insight to His disciples while leaving others in the dark: "To you it has been given to know the secrets of the kingdom of heaven, but to them it has not been given" (Matthew 13:11). He taught them to pray for the coming of the kingdom, "Your kingdom come, your will be done, on earth as it is in heaven" (Matthew 6:10), and assured them that they would share in its blessings: "You are those who have stayed with me in my trials, and I assign to you, as my Father assigned to me, a kingdom, that you may eat and drink at my table in my kingdom and sit on thrones judging the twelve tribes of Israel" (Luke 22:28-30). He also spoke of the kingdom's ultimate fulfillment, saying, "When the Son of Man comes in his glory, and all the angels with him, then he will sit on his glorious throne" (Matthew 25:31).

Jesus was profoundly committed to teaching His disciples the importance of prioritizing the kingdom of God, warning them against divided loyalties. In Matthew 6, He clearly underscores that a heart invested in earthly pursuits cannot truly belong to the kingdom. Jesus set a firm boundary, stating, "No one can serve two masters, for either he will hate the one and love the other, or he will be devoted to the one and despise the other" (Matthew 6:24). The kingdom calls for undivided allegiance, urging believers to seek God's will wholeheartedly and live to glorify Him alone.

At the heart of the gospel is Jesus' powerful command in Matthew 6:33: "Seek first the kingdom of God." Here, Jesus emphasizes that God is deeply concerned with the priorities of His followers' hearts. The gospel calls for total commitment to the kingdom, inviting believers to make it their ultimate motivation and guiding principle in life.

The desert fathers, such as Saint Anthony, modeled this commitment through their simple, devoted lives, demonstrating that the kingdom of God is accessible to all who seek it earnestly. Saint Anthony expressed this truth, saying,

> Some leave home and cross the seas in order to gain an education, but there is no need for us to go away on account of the kingdom of God nor need we cross the sea in search of virtue. For the Lord has told us, "The kingdom of God is within you." All that is needed for goodness is that which is within, the human heart.[1]

In sum, Jesus taught that entering the kingdom of God requires more than just outward obedience; it demands a complete transformation of the heart and a life wholly devoted to seeking and glorifying God.

RIGHTEOUSNESS

Jesus frequently spoke about righteousness because it is the characteristic that matters most to God. Righteousness is the key criterion that determines whether a person can enter the kingdom of God. In the Sermon on the Mount, Jesus emphasized that this righteousness must surpass that of the scribes and Pharisees. He declared, "For I tell you, unless your righteousness exceeds that of the scribes and Pharisees, you will never enter the kingdom of heaven" (Matthew 5:20). The scribes and Pharisees were devoted to living righteously as professional students of religion, committed to studying the scriptures and adhering to their teachings. Yet, Jesus taught that the righteousness required for entry into the kingdom must go beyond mere external compliance—it demands a standard of purity that addresses the very heart of human motives.

The kingdom of God operates on principles that are distinct from those of the world. God's concern is not merely with outward acts of sin but with the condition of the human heart. Righteousness in God's kingdom is rooted in love and is free from selfish motives; it is a standard of character that can only be attained through experiencing God's reign in one's life. In essence, the kingdom provides what it requires—true righteousness.

Theologian Martin Luther grappled with the concept of righteousness, particularly the idea of how sinners could obtain a righteousness acceptable to a holy God.[2] C. S. Lewis similarly wrestled with the human condition, acknowledging humanity's inherent flaws. Reflecting on his own shortcomings, he wrote, "In my most clear-sighted moments not only do I not think myself a nice man, but I know that I am a very nasty one. I can look at some of the things I have done with horror and loathing."[3] Luther ultimately found resolution in the gospel, which offers justifying righteousness to believers. This revelation led him to understand God not as a harsh judge, but as merciful and gracious, extending righteousness to sinners as a divine gift.

Theologian Wayne Grudem defines righteousness as "the doctrine that God always acts in accordance with what is right and that he is himself the final standard of what is right."[4] God embodies righteousness, and He alone has the authority to declare what is right. In Isaiah 45:19, God says, "I the Lord speak the truth; I declare what is right." Moses also proclaimed God's justice and uprightness in Deuteronomy 32:4: "All his ways are justice. A God of faithfulness and without iniquity, just and upright is he."

God's justice requires that He addresses sin by administering the consequences that individuals rightfully deserve. Because of His righteous nature, God cannot overlook sin; doing so would contradict His very character. The only way God can justly refrain from punishing sin is through the substitutionary sacrifice of Christ. The Apostle Paul reveals that God sent Christ as a sacrificial offering to bear the penalty of sin, writing:

> For all have sinned and fall short of the glory of God, and are justified by his grace as a gift, through the redemption that is Christ Jesus, whom God put forward as a propitiation by his blood, to be received by faith. This was to show God's righteousness, because in his divine forbearance he had passed over former sins. It was to show his righteousness at the present time, so that he might be just and the justifier of the one who has faith in Jesus (Romans 3:23-26).

Through this powerful passage, Paul emphasizes that God's righteousness is revealed in His grace—offered freely to all who believe in Christ, who bore the weight of humanity's sin. This act demonstrates not only God's justice but also His mercy, as He alone justifies those who place their faith in Jesus.

Biblical scholars Merrill C. Tenney and Moisés Silva define righteousness as "morally right behavior or character—justice, honesty, loyalty," and further explain that "righteousness represents any conformity to a standard, whether that standard pertains to the inner character of a person or the objective standard of accepted law. With reference to a person, it has to do with his conformity to God's holiness."[5] God stands as the ultimate standard of righteousness; therefore, true righteousness is measured by alignment with His moral character.

However, human attempts at righteousness, when based solely on absolute obedience, inevitably fall short. It is only through God's mercy and righteousness, extended to humanity through the forgiveness of sins, that people can be justified. In Christ, God's righteousness becomes the believer's own, obtained through a relationship of faith. The anonymous early Christian author, Mathetes, beautifully describes this sacrificial exchange:

He himself took on him the burden of our iniquities, he gave his own Son as a ransom for us, the holy One for transgressors, the blameless One for the wicked, the righteous One for the unrighteous, the incorruptible One for the corruptible, the immortal One for them that are mortal. For what other thing was capable of covering our sins than His righteousness? By what other one was it possible that we, the wicked and ungodly, could be justified, than by the only Son of God? O sweet exchange! O unsearchable operation! O benefits surpassing all expectation! That the wickedness of many should be hid in a single righteous One, and that righteousness of One should justify many transgressors![6]

Righteousness, then, is not something to be earned but rather a relationship of dependence on Jesus, the source of all righteousness. Tenney and Silva affirm this truth, stating, "Christian righteousness is never an attainment; it is a direction, a loyalty, a commitment, a hope—and only someday an arrival."[7]

Throughout scripture, righteousness is portrayed as a life fully committed to God, characterized by obedience to His commandments and a love for others that goes beyond self-interest. This steadfast devotion is essential for entering the kingdom of God. The Apostle Paul emphasizes this truth in 1 Corinthians 6:9, warning, "Do you not know that the unrighteous will not inherit the kingdom of God?" In the Old Testament, God's expectations for righteous living are vividly illustrated, especially in the Psalms. David asks,

"Who shall ascend the hill of the Lord? And who shall stand in his holy place? He who has clean hands and a pure heart, who does not lift up his soul to what is false and does not swear deceitfully" (Psalm 24:3-4). In Psalm 51, he further proclaims, "Behold, you delight in truth in the inward being, and you teach me wisdom in the secret heart" (Psalm 51:6). These passages reveal the deep integrity, purity, and truthfulness that God seeks in those who pursue His ways.

Righteousness is not attained through religious acts or achieving moral standards but through standing before God with a heart that is both clean and sincere in its motives. In His mercy, God provides righteousness for believers through Christ. As the Apostle Paul explains in 2 Corinthians 5:21, "For our sake he made him to be sin who knew no sin, so that in him we might become the righteousness of God." When individuals are born again, Christ removes their sins and imparts His righteousness to them, bringing peace, joy, and the assurance of being God's children. This transformation underscores the power of the gospel, which offers not only forgiveness but also the restoration of righteousness in the lives of believers.

POWER

In 1 Corinthians 4:20, the Apostle Paul emphasizes to Timothy the vital role of God's power in living a life aligned with the kingdom of God. He states, "For the kingdom of God does not consist in talk but in power." The kingdom is more than just words of encouragement or wise counsel; it is a divine power that can cast out demons, perform miracles, and bring about real change in people's lives. This power is not only accessible to individual believers but is also meant to be wielded for the work of the kingdom. The preaching of the gospel is not merely a message; it is a proclamation of God's power to save souls from the kingdom of darkness. Paul reinforces this powerful truth in Romans 1:16, declaring, "For I am not ashamed of the Gospel, for it is the power of God for salvation to everyone who believes, to the Jew first and also to the Greek."

The Power and Authority of Jesus

The authority and power that Jesus exemplified were unmistakable, particularly evident after His Sermon on the Mount: "And when Jesus finished these sayings, the crowds were astonished at his teaching, for he was teaching them as one who had authority, and not as their scribes" (Matthew 7:28-29). Unlike other teachers who relied on the authority of others, Jesus spoke with inherent authority. As the embodiment of the kingdom of God, power was a defining characteristic of everything He said and did. Jesus' authority was evident in the signs and miracles He performed—giving sight to the blind, healing the sick and deaf, and even raising the dead. When He sent out the seventy-two disciples into ministry, He instructed them, "Whenever you enter a town and they receive you, eat what is set before you. Heal the sick in it and say to them, 'The kingdom of God has come near you'" (Luke 10:8-9). These healings were tangible evidence of the kingdom's power at work. The ultimate display of Jesus' power was His resurrection, which triumphed over death and the grave.

A significant aspect of Jesus' ministry was the casting out of demons, a clear and powerful demonstration of the kingdom's authority over darkness. George Eldon Ladd, in *The Gospel of the Kingdom*, explains the significance of this display of power, writing,

> What means the announcement that the Kingdom of God has come near? It is this: that God is now acting among men to deliver them from bondage to Satan. It is the announcement that God, in the person of Christ, is doing something—if you please, is attacking the very kingdom of Satan himself. The exorcism of demons is proof that the Kingdom of God has come among men and is at work among them. The casting out of demons is itself a work of the Kingdom of God.[8]

Jesus Himself affirmed this, saying, "But if it is by the Spirit of God that I cast out demons, then the kingdom of God has come upon you" (Matthew 12:28). This supernatural power demonstrated that the kingdom of God had broken into the present world, binding Satan's influence and freeing humanity to experience the blessings of life in the kingdom.

The spiritual authority that flows from Christ's reign within His followers enables victory over every evil force. As early Christian theologian Origen observed, this victory over the reign of sin is made possible through the indwelling kingdom of God within each believer.[9]

The Power of Pentecost

The day of Pentecost marked the arrival of the Holy Spirit's power upon the disciples. Acts 2:1-4 describes the event:

> When the day of Pentecost arrived, they were all together in one place. And suddenly there came from heaven a sound like a mighty rushing wind, and it filled the entire house where they were sitting. And divided tongues as of fire appeared to them and rested on each one of them. And they were filled with the Holy Spirit and began to speak in other tongues as the Spirit gave them utterance.

When the kingdom of God descends upon a person, the supernatural power of the kingdom falls onto them through the empowerment of the Spirit. This Spirit-power emboldens believers to witness for Christ and proclaim the gospel, as seen in Peter's first sermon after Pentecost. Filled with this divine power, Peter delivered his sermon with such authority and conviction that it pierced the hearts of his listeners, resulting in a radical transformation in their lives. Acts 2:41-43 records the outcome:

> So those who received his word were baptized, and there were added that day about three thousand souls. And they devoted themselves to the apostles' teaching and the fellowship, to the breaking of bread and the prayers. And awe came upon every soul, and many wonders and signs were being done through the apostles.

The power of the kingdom of God stirs a deep conviction of sin, compelling individuals to make a decisive commitment to Christ, as vividly demonstrated by the response to Peter's sermon. This kingdom power equips individuals to comprehend and embrace the gospel message, as Paul explains, "Now we have received not the spirit of the world, but the Spirit who is from God, that we might understand the things freely given us by God" (1 Corinthians 2:12). It is the power that brings new life, transforming what was once dead into something vibrant and alive. Paul further emphasizes this transformation: "Therefore, if anyone is in Christ, he is a new creation. The old has passed away; behold, the new has come" (2 Corinthians 5:17). The kingdom of God equips believers with the power to overcome every challenge, affirming that "in all these things we are more than conquerors through him who loved us" (Romans 8:37).

THE KINGDOM OF GOD MISUNDERSTOOD BY THE EARLY CHURCH

The first-century church faced significant challenges as it struggled to grasp the true nature of the kingdom of God. Leadership crises, heresy, division, arrogance, and immoral behavior plagued these early Christian communities. The apostles addressed these critical issues through letters, offering guidance and correction to the fledgling churches.

One of the most notable examples of misunderstanding occurred in the church at Corinth. Composed primarily of Gentiles who had converted from paganism, the Corinthian church continued to embrace a Hellenistic worldview, particularly in matters of ethical behavior. Instead of influencing their city for the kingdom of God, their attitudes and conduct mirrored the sinful lifestyle of the surrounding culture. Some leaders within the church exacerbated the problem by challenging Paul's authority and distorting the gospel to align with Hellenistic values. These corrupt leaders wielded significant influence, leading the congregation astray. In his letter to the Corinthians, Paul sought to reassert his authority and correct the church's wayward theology and behavior. He reminded them that as Christians, they were to follow his example as he followed Christ, the embodiment of the kingdom of God. Paul urged the Corinthians to abandon their imitation of secular culture and instead model their beliefs and behaviors after Christ Himself. The church in Corinth struggled with pride, embraced secular values, altered the gospel, and dishonored Paul's authority. In his letter, Paul also directly addressed the church leaders, emphasizing the importance of humility and faithful service. He urged them to see themselves as servants of Christ, accountable to God, and entrusted with the responsibility of stewarding their positions with integrity.

In his letter to the Galatians, Paul addressed similar concerns, focusing on the false teachers who had infiltrated the churches in Galatia. These individuals questioned Paul's authority and undermined his credibility, leading many of his converts away from the truth. The Galatians, demonstrating their instability and lack of confidence in the gospel, swiftly abandoned the truth in favor of a distorted doctrine that prioritized human effort and merit over divine grace. Paul's letter was a direct response to this crisis, as he sought to reaffirm the true gospel and restore the faith of his converts.

The Apostle John also confronted significant challenges in his letters, particularly during a time of spiritual confusion when beliefs contrary to orthodox Christian doctrine were infiltrating the church. John's letters, written with pastoral care, encouraged his readers that their eternal life was secure because they knew God in Christ. He addressed issues of right belief about Jesus, a proper attitude toward sin, and relationships characterized by love. In his second and third letters, John warned against false teachers—whom he described as deceivers, false prophets, and antichrists—who had left his church and were spreading heretical doctrines. He wrote, "For many deceivers have gone out into the world, those who do not confess the coming of Jesus Christ in the flesh. Such a one is the deceiver and antichrist" (2 John 7). John instructed the churches against showing hospitality to these heretics to prevent their false teachings from infecting the Christian communities. These false teachers promoted worldly ideologies, lacked genuine love, and showed a disregard for righteousness. Recognizing this threat, John urged the churches to remember the importance of holy living and steadfast obedience to God's commands, reinforcing the necessity of safeguarding their faith.

The early church's failure to prioritize God's reign, rule, and sovereignty led to the creation of their own kingdoms, shaped by secular cultural values. Paul described these worldly values as "works of the flesh," which included sexual immorality, impurity, sensuality, idolatry, jealousy, sorcery, enmity, strife, jealousy, fits of anger, rivalries, dissensions, divisions, envy, drunkenness, orgies, and other sinful behaviors. He warned that those who engaged in such practices would not inherit the kingdom of God.

Satan's influence infiltrated the early Christian communities, blinding them to the light of the gospel and drawing them into rebellion against God. As a result, they failed to grasp the truths of scripture, creating a version of the gospel shaped by their own understanding. Rather than embodying the example of Jesus—who lived as the kingdom of God incarnate, displaying holiness, righteousness, love, and selflessness—the church reflected the world, becoming preoccupied with earthly concerns. By embracing secular cultural values, the church lost its distinctiveness, failing to serve as the "salt of the earth" that Jesus called it to be. As Jesus warned, salt that loses its saltiness is "no longer good for anything except to be thrown out and trampled under people's feet" (Matthew 5:13). In this way, the early church had become tasteless salt, ineffective in its calling to advance the kingdom of God.

The first-century church's struggle to understand the principles of the kingdom of God was evident in their adoption of secular attitudes and behaviors. Immorality thrived, and false teachings gained ground due to the powerful influence of corrupt leaders. Amma Syncletica, a desert mother, cautioned against the seductive allure of worldly pleasures, reminding believers that true satisfaction comes from spiritual disciplines, not material abundance. She wrote,

> Do not let yourself be seduced by the delights of the riches of the world, as though they contained something useful on account of vain pleasure. Worldly people esteem the culinary art, but you, through fasting and thanks to cheap food, go beyond their abundance of food. It is written: "He who is sated loathes honey" (Proverbs 27:7). Do not fill yourself with bread and you will not desire wine.[10]

The early church grappled with a pull toward worldly pleasures, which gradually dulled their desire for the kingdom of God. Immoral attitudes and behaviors began to shape their lives, diverting them from authentic discipleship. As kingdom ambassadors, the apostles were tasked with confronting the abuse of leadership and unethical behavior within these Christian communities. They held the crucial responsibility of steering these churches back to the foundational truths of the gospel of Christ, reminding them that their true allegiance was to the kingdom of God, not to the fleeting pleasures of the world.

LIVING OUT THE CHARACTERISTICS OF THE KINGDOM OF GOD

The kingdom of God, as revealed through the life and teachings of Jesus, presents a radically different way of life, one that is centered on righteousness, submission to God's rule, and empowered by divine authority. The kingdom is not merely a future hope but a present reality, demanding a response from all believers. Jesus embodied the kingdom, living a life fully dedicated to glorifying the Father, demonstrating kingdom power, and inviting others into a transformative relationship with God.

The key characteristics of the kingdom of God—righteousness, seeking the kingdom, divine power and authority, and a deep relationship with the Father—serve as a model for how Christians are called to live. Jesus' mission was not only to reveal the kingdom but also to demonstrate how His followers should embody its values in every aspect of their lives. His teachings continue to challenge believers to seek the kingdom above all else, rejecting worldly influences in favor of a life aligned with God's will.

The early church struggled with misunderstandings about the kingdom, often succumbing to secular influences and moral failings. Yet, the message of the kingdom remains clear: to live under God's sovereign reign, striving for righteousness, and empowered by the Spirit. By embracing these characteristics of the kingdom, believers can continue Jesus' mission, advancing His reign in the world and living as true citizens of the kingdom of God.

The early church's failure to fully comprehend the kingdom of God resulted in misunderstandings that undermined its mission and effectiveness. Unfortunately, this challenge persists today, as many pastors and ministry leaders still struggle with the same issues. Like their predecessors, many modern church leaders are often seduced by the allure of secular success, power, and cultural relevance, allowing these influences to distort their understanding of God's kingdom. Despite centuries of church history, the church continues to repeat the same mistakes, failing to learn from the past.

Pastors and ministry leaders have a critical responsibility to rediscover and realign their leadership with the principles of the kingdom of God. Ministry should never be shaped by worldly values or measured by secular standards of success. Instead, leaders must wholeheartedly embrace Christ-centered leadership—anchored in righteousness, submission to God's will, and the empowering presence of the Holy Spirit.

Only through this realignment can they faithfully shepherd their congregations and advance the church's true mission. The mistakes of the past don't have to dictate the future, but change will only come if ministry leaders choose to prioritize the kingdom of God over the values of the world.

Chapter Six

KINGDOM LEADERSHIP

Urgency, Transformation, and
the Cost of Discipleship

THE URGENCY AND TRANSFORMATION OF KINGDOM LIVING

IN MARK 1:14-15, as Jesus enters Galilee, He announces the gospel message with compelling urgency: "The time is fulfilled, and the kingdom of God is at hand; *repent* and believe in the gospel." This proclamation underscores the urgency of the kingdom's arrival and the transformative power it demands. The term *repentance* speaks to a deep, intentional change of mind, a shift that alters the very direction of one's life. This transformation isn't merely a surface-level decision but a radical reorientation—from a life centered on self or sin to one centered on God and Christ. Jesus calls His followers to embrace this profound change, urging them to move from self-centeredness to Christ-centeredness. Embracing this call means more than a change of thoughts or intentions; it requires a life wholly surrendered to the priorities and purposes of God's kingdom.

Jesus makes it clear that embracing the kingdom of God necessitates change; it is impossible to pursue the kingdom and remain unchanged. Choosing the kingdom involves turning away from selfish pursuits and wholeheartedly embracing a life of righteousness in Christ. The urgency of this decision is clearly illustrated in the way Jesus called His disciples. When He said, "Follow me," they immediately abandoned their previous lives and followed Him, recognizing in Him the very embodiment of the kingdom.

Luke 9:57-62 further highlights the seriousness of this choice. Jesus challenges those expressing a desire to follow Him, declaring, "Leave the dead to bury their own dead. But as for you, go and proclaim the kingdom of God." He then adds, "No one who puts his hand to the plow and looks back is fit for the kingdom of God." These statements emphasize the total allegiance and loyalty required to pursue the kingdom, even at great personal cost. Choosing the kingdom of God often involves sacrifice, including the risk of death or rejection by others. However, followers of Christ are called to maintain their focus on the reign of Christ and the coming kingdom, enabling them to endure present challenges. The decision to follow Jesus is both urgent and sacrificial, embodying the same commitment to the kingdom's mission that Jesus Himself demonstrated in His life and death.

SALT AND LIGHT

In the Gospel of Matthew, Jesus tells His disciples,

You are the salt of the earth, but if salt has lost its taste, how shall its saltiness be restored? It is no longer good for anything except to be thrown out and trampled under people's feet (Matthew 5:13).

Here, Jesus emphasizes that those who reject the principles of the kingdom are like salt that has lost its flavor—useless and discarded. Craig Keener notes, "Just as tasteless salt lacks value to the person who uses it, so does a professed disciple without genuine commitment prove valueless for the work of the kingdom."[1] Saltiness refers to a person's character, which is developed by embracing God's principles. Kingdom people must embody this "saltiness" to impact the world for the kingdom of God. Just as salt enhances and transforms the taste of food, followers of Jesus are called to influence and reshape the culture around them.

Jesus continues this metaphor in Matthew 5:14-16, saying,

You are the light of the world. A city set on a hill cannot be hidden. Nor do people light a lamp and put it under a basket, but on a stand, and it gives light to all in the house. In the same way, let your light shine before others, so that they may see your good works and give glory to your Father who is in heaven.

Here, Jesus communicates that if His disciples' lives do not reflect the principles of the kingdom, they are ineffective in their mission. Their character must radiate the kingdom's values; otherwise, they become useless. Jesus sets a high standard for the character of His followers.

Living as salt and light in the world means embodying a way of life that is distinct from the surrounding culture. It involves striving to emulate the righteousness that Jesus modeled, resulting in a genuine transformation of the heart from worldly values to the values of the kingdom of God. Bible scholar John Stott emphasizes this expectation set by Jesus for His disciples: "They were not to take their cue from the people around them, but from him, and so prove to be genuine children of their heavenly Father."[2] Jesus calls His followers to a higher standard of living, one that is distinctively different—a Christian counterculture that stands as a beacon of the kingdom in the world today.

THE COUNTERCULTURAL NATURE OF KINGDOM LEADERSHIP

Jesus' proclamation of the kingdom of God stirred controversy among the New Testament community of believers. His message clashed with their long-standing expectations, challenging their deeply rooted beliefs and assumptions. The principles of God's kingdom are often demanding and counter to conventional thinking. Robert Wayne Stacy aptly notes, "There is always a *counter*cultural character to the kingdom, its participants being at once *in* the world but not *of* it."³

In the kingdom of God, leadership is not defined by worldly values; rather, it stands in stark contrast to them. A leader in God's kingdom embodies a countercultural approach—serving as a first-follower, representative, and ambassador of Jesus in His physical absence. All power and authority for such leaders is derived solely from Christ, with no room for independent rights or self-derived authority. True kingdom leaders operate in ways that reflect life under God's reign, continually directing others toward His kingdom. Stacy insightfully explains, "Leaders, therefore, are living, breathing intimations of the kingdom, foreshadowing in this world the vision and values of that world. They are 'kingdom guides,' and as such express 'leadership' appropriate to the new reality in which they live."⁴

Jesus selected twelve disciples as leaders, setting them apart to represent His mission and empowering them with His authority. These chosen men were specifically trained by Jesus to fulfill a unique role of leadership and authority. His teachings to them served as foundational leadership instruction, equipping the apostles to spread the good news of the kingdom and perform miracles. Luke 9:1-2 captures this commissioning: "And he called the twelve together and gave them power and authority over all demons and to cure diseases, and he sent them out to proclaim the kingdom of God and to heal."

Jesus tailored His teachings specifically for this group of leaders, placing profound trust in them as He prepared them to carry on His ministry and mission after His departure. These teachings underscored the true cost of living according to kingdom principles, a path that demanded complete commitment. Scholar Douglas Petersen writes, "Life under the new rule of God required a dramatic change in the rules of leadership."[5] For Jesus, the standards for kingdom leadership were exceptionally high, requiring His followers to embrace a deep level of dedication. His disciples were challenged to count the cost, setting aside worldly attachments to fully commit to a life shaped by the cross.

EMBRACING THE CROSS: THE COST OF KINGDOM LEADERSHIP

The disciples, though committed to the kingdom of God, were not immune to worldly temptations as leaders. They struggled to understand the kingdom apart from the prevailing cultural values, often interpreting success in terms of status and authority rather than through the lens of the cross. They did not initially grasp the cost inherent in true discipleship. Following Jesus required them to embrace the cross and its demands fully.

Jesus clarified this call when addressing both His disciples and the crowd in Mark 8:34-35: "If anyone would come after me, let him deny himself and take up his cross and follow me. For whoever would save his life will lose it, but whoever loses his life for my sake and the gospel's will save it." This teaching underscores that the way of the cross calls for a life of self-denial and suffering, requiring one to let go of control and surrender fully to God.

Stacy reinforces this idea, stating, "For the disciple, for the leader, following Jesus means giving up any pretense that we are 'in charge.'"[6] Kingdom leadership is characterized by the countercultural life that Jesus modeled. Leaders are called to surrender their ego and selfish ambitions, embracing the suffering and sacrifice represented by the cross.

SERVANT LEADERSHIP IN THE KINGDOM OF GOD

Jesus redefined leadership through the transformative lens of service. In Mark 10:45, He offers a profound lesson on what true leadership entails. When James and John requested positions of prominence in the kingdom, Jesus responded, "For even the Son of Man came not to be served but to serve, and to give his life as a ransom for many." The two brothers sought ambition and self-promotion, but Jesus sharply rebuked them, illustrating that the path of the cross is defined by humility and selfless service. Biblical scholar Alan Cole observes, "So Jesus justly rebukes both the two and then ten at once, by showing them their common ignorance of the very nature of Christian leadership. All such leadership is only humble service, for it takes its colour from the example of Jesus, who is above all, the Servant."[7]

Jesus established a clear distinction between worldly authority and kingdom leadership when He said, "But it shall not be so among you" (Mark 10:43). Kingdom leadership is rooted in sacrifice and service to others, which is the true measure of greatness in God's eyes. Gene Wilkes, professor of New Testament and Leadership, affirms, "This example of Jesus does not fit the cultural picture of leadership. Jesus, however, did not come to show us a better way to do things. He came to show us how to live as kingdom people."[8]

In the first century, secular leaders exercised power primarily to serve their own interests, using authority as a tool to assert dominance and fulfill personal ambitions. This mindset fostered a leadership culture rooted in control, ego, and self-promotion rather than humility and service. Leaders leveraged their influence to maintain power over others, prioritizing their status above all else. Jesus confronted this mindset head-on, challenging the traditional leadership norms that His disciples had come to accept. His teachings redefined authority, calling for a radical shift away from the prevailing cultural standards. Kingdom leadership, as demonstrated by Jesus, is built on principles of selfless service and sacrificial love, in sharp contrast to the self-centered pursuit of power. Reflecting on this new paradigm, Douglas Petersen explains, "What happens to Jesus will happen to his followers, too. The disciples must learn that for them, as for Jesus, leadership is service, defeat is victory, and death is the pathway to life."[9] Jesus' model set a new standard for leadership—one that prioritizes kingdom values over worldly ambition, demanding a deep transformation of heart, character, and purpose.

LEADING LIKE JESUS: THE KINGDOM FRAMEWORK

Jesus embodied the kingdom of God, living a life that perfectly reflected its values—serving as the ultimate example of a kingdom leader. Jesus set apart the apostles specifically to train them in the ways of kingdom leadership. He spent forty days after His resurrection teaching them about the kingdom, as recorded in Acts 1:3: "He presented himself alive to them after his suffering by many proofs, appearing to them during forty days and speaking about the kingdom of God." For Jesus, the kingdom of God was of paramount importance, and He commanded His followers to seek it first in their lives.

Leaders in the kingdom of God are called to prioritize the kingdom and the righteousness of Jesus in every aspect of their lives, submitting fully to God's rule and authority. The kingdom of God is meant to serve as the guiding framework for all other priorities, shaping every decision and action. This command is as relevant today as it was for the apostles. Kingdom leaders do not seek personal notoriety or build their own empires; instead, they recognize Jesus as the only reigning King. Jesus emphasized this principle in Matthew 6:24, saying, "No one can serve two masters, for either he will hate the one and love the other, or he will be devoted to the one and despise the other." Leaders who do not make Jesus their Master are inevitably drawn to serve their own interests. Pastor and theologian Jeremy Treat emphasizes this perspective, noting, "When we don't give *everything* over to

Jesus, we're still the one who is in control. We act as our own king and then try to use Jesus to accomplish our goals."[10]

Kingdom leadership permeates all areas of a leader's life, shaping their character and guiding their behavior. Leaders who are truly committed to Christ and His mission aim to glorify God in all things, as reflected in Romans 11:36: "For from him and through him and to him are all things. To him be glory forever" (Romans 11:36). Treat encourages leaders to move beyond building personal kingdoms, urging them to focus on the one pursuit that truly matters—the kingdom of God. He writes, "To experience the life Jesus says we were made for, we need to have kingdom perspective, live with kingdom purpose, and learn to be kingdom people."[11] This perspective challenges leaders to prioritize God's kingdom above all else, allowing it to shape their purpose and legacy.

EMBRACING KINGDOM LEADERSHIP: A CALL TO TRANSFORMATION AND SERVICE

This chapter emphasizes the transformative and countercultural nature of kingdom leadership, deeply rooted in Jesus' urgent call to live under God's reign. Kingdom leadership demands not only personal transformation but also a radical reorientation of values, aligning fully with the principles Jesus exemplified—servanthood, humility, and total submission to God's will. The cost of true discipleship is high, involving a willingness to embrace the cross, forsake selfish ambition, and commit to living as salt and light within a world often shaped by conflicting values.

Kingdom leaders, as demonstrated by Jesus and His teachings, must prioritize the kingdom above all else, recognizing that true leadership is not about wielding power or authority but about serving others and leading by example. The path to greatness in God's kingdom is marked by humility, service, and self-denial—qualities at the heart of Jesus' ministry. By following His example, leaders are entrusted with the mission to embody the kingdom in their own lives and lead others with the same dedication to God's purposes.

Ultimately, kingdom leadership is a call to surrender, transformation, and urgency, where leaders are entrusted with cultivating a kingdom-centered mindset that prioritizes God's sovereign rule in every dimension of life. In today's world, the challenge for leaders is to remain steadfast in upholding kingdom values, fully embracing the transformative power of the gospel, and leading others into the life of discipleship that Jesus Himself exemplified.

PSALM 23

The Lord is my shepherd; I shall not want.

He makes me lie down in green pastures.

He leads me beside still waters.

He restores my soul.

He leads me in paths of righteousness for his name's sake.

Even though I walk through the valley

of the shadow of death,

I will fear no evil, for you are with me;

your rod and your staff, they comfort me.

You prepare a table before me

in the presence of my enemies;

you anoint my head with oil; my cup overflows.

Surely goodness and mercy shall follow me

all the days of my life,

and I shall dwell in the house of the Lord forever.

THE GOOD SHEPHERD DISCOURSE

"Truly, truly, I say to you, he who does not enter the sheepfold by the door but climbs in by another way, that man is a thief and a robber. But he who enters by the door is the shepherd of the sheep. To him the gatekeeper opens. The sheep hear his voice, and he calls his own sheep by name and leads them out. When he has brought out all his own, he goes before them, and the sheep follow him, for they know his voice. A stranger they will not follow, but they will flee from him, for they do not know the voice of strangers." This figure of speech Jesus used with them, but they did not understand what he was saying to them.

So Jesus again said to them, "Truly, truly, I say to you, I am the door of the sheep. All who came before me are thieves and robbers, but the sheep did not listen to them. I am the door. If anyone enters by me, he will be saved and will go in and out and find pasture. The thief comes only to steal and kill and destroy. I came that they may have life and have it abundantly. I am the good shepherd. The good shepherd lays down his life for the sheep. He who is a hired hand and not a shepherd, who does not own the sheep, sees the wolf coming and leaves the sheep and flees, and the wolf snatches them and scatters them. He flees because he is a hired hand and cares nothing for the sheep. I am the good shepherd. I know my own and my own know me, just as the Father knows me and I know the Father; and I lay down my life for the sheep. And I have other sheep that are not of this fold. I must bring them also, and they will listen to my voice. So there will be one flock, one shepherd. For this reason the Father loves me, because I lay down my life that I may take it up again. No one takes from me, but I lay it down of my own accord. I have authority to lay it down, and I have authority to take it up again. This charge I have received from my Father."

There was again a division among the Jews because of these words. Many of them said, "He has a demon, and is insane; why listen to him?" Others said, "These are not the words of one who is oppressed by a demon. Can a demon open the eyes of the blind?"

- John 10:1-21

Chapter Seven

A BIBLICAL MODEL OF LEADERSHIP

Shepherd Leadership

EMBRACING SHEPHERD LEADERSHIP AS A MODEL FOR KINGDOM LEADERSHIP

THE METAPHOR OF THE SHEPHERD, deeply rooted in the Old Testament, provides a powerful image of leadership that extends throughout scripture. This role is far more than a simple pastoral duty; it embodies a deep connection between leader and follower, symbolizing the divine care and guidance God offers His people. In ancient Israel, shepherding involved not only guiding and protecting the flock but also demonstrating a deep commitment to their well-being. This image of leadership, grounded in servanthood and responsibility, sets the foundation for understanding kingdom leadership as presented in the Bible.

Shepherd leadership is characterized by a balance of strength and tenderness, reflecting the leader's commitment to the welfare of those under their care. The role requires vigilance, courage, and compassion, ensuring that the flock is fed, protected, and guided. In this model, leadership is not about power or authority but about serving others with a heart attuned to God's will. The leader acts as a steward, accountable to God for the care of His people, and must embody the qualities of a true shepherd: humility, sacrifice, and unwavering dedication.

The concept of shepherd leadership is further developed through the life and ministry of Jesus, who is presented in the New Testament as the Good Shepherd. Jesus not only taught about the qualities of a good shepherd but lived them out, setting the ultimate example for leaders in God's kingdom. His life of service, sacrifice, and love for the flock models the type of leadership that God desires for His people. Jesus' actions and teachings reveal that true leadership involves laying down one's life for others, prioritizing their needs above one's own, and leading with a heart fully devoted to God.

This chapter explores the biblical model of shepherd leadership, drawing from the Old Testament's rich imagery and the New Testament's portrayal of Jesus as the Good Shepherd. By examining a shepherd's responsibilities, challenges, and characteristics, insights are gained into what it means to lead in God's kingdom. Shepherd leaders are called to emulate the heart of God, caring for His people with the same love, compassion, and dedication that He demonstrates. This model challenges contemporary notions of leadership by emphasizing service, sacrifice, and a deep, personal connection with those who are led.

THE SHEPHERD MOTIF: A FOUNDATION FOR KINGDOM LEADERSHIP

The biblical metaphor of a shepherd, originating in the Old Testament, provides a foundational image of leadership. The term "shepherd" can be understood in three primary ways, whether expressed as the verbs "shepherding," "tending," or "herding," or as the nouns "shepherd," "shepherdess," or "herdsman." These applications refer to herders of livestock, YHWH as the Shepherd of Israel, or individuals and groups serving as leaders or rulers. When used metaphorically, "shepherd" in the Old Testament often carries royal connotations, suggesting a connection with kingship. This association, as noted in the *NIV Cultural Backgrounds Study Bible*, is common in the ancient Near East, where monarchy was often viewed through the lens of shepherding. In this context, royal authority was understood to belong to God, with the king acting as God's representative. The people, seen as God's flock, were entrusted to the king, who was accountable to God for their care.[1]

Shepherding in the Old Testament required a balance of strong leadership and tender care. Sheep were entirely dependent on their shepherd, needing his guidance and protection for survival. True shepherds were defined by their wholehearted commitment and genuine concern for their flock. They took responsibility for every aspect of the sheep's well-being—from feeding and safety to finding and restoring lost sheep. The relationship between the shepherd and the flock was intimate, built on trust and dedication. Shepherding was a demanding role, requiring both toughness and resolve to lead sheep through challenging terrain and protect them from dangers. It involved a balance of bold leadership and nurturing care, demonstrating courage and strength.

THE CONCEPT OF SHEPHERD LEADERSHIP

The Hebrew word "nagiyd," meaning "leader," is closely linked to the idea of shepherd leadership. This term embodies servanthood and signifies someone who submits to a higher authority. Key elements in the root meaning of "nagiyd" include standing out boldly, announcing, and manifesting. God desires leaders—nagiyd leaders—who will shepherd His people with a heart of submission to His authority, listening to His will, and faithfully carrying it out with the empowerment of divine authority. These leaders are obedient and set an example for others through their dedication to God and His commands. David, described as a man after God's own heart, is a prime example of a nagiyd leader in Israel (1 Samuel 13:14).

Throughout both the Old and New Testaments, titles such as bishop, presbyter, priest, preacher, minister, and shepherd are used to describe God's leaders. Yet historically, "shepherd" has been among the least commonly applied titles within the church. Frank Damazio, theologian, pastor, and leadership coach, notes that while many church leaders bear this title, few fully embody or practice true shepherding. When the function of a shepherd is neglected within the church, the result is a lack of genuine and loving spiritual care for the congregation. It is vital for God's leaders to possess the heart of a shepherd, prioritizing the flock's well-being above their own needs.[2]

Psalm 23 vividly illustrates a leader who goes before the sheep, guiding them safely and providing for their needs. W. Phillip Keller captures this image of the ever-present shepherd in his book, *A Shepherd Looks at Psalm 23*, where he writes:

> It is the alertness, the awareness, the diligence of a never-tiring master which alone assures the sheep of excellent care. And from the sheep's standpoint it is knowing that the shepherd is there; it is the constant awareness of his presence nearby that automatically eliminates most of the difficulties and dangers while at the same time providing a sense of security and serenity. It is the sheep owner's presence that guarantees there will be no lack of any sort; that there will be abundant green pastures; that there will be still, clean waters; that there will be new paths into fresh fields; that there will be safe summers on the high table lands; that there will be freedom from fear; that there will be antidotes for the flies and disease and parasites; that there will be quietness and contentment.[3]

THE BIBLICAL METAPHOR OF SHEPHERD AS LEADERSHIP

Scripture consistently uses the shepherd metaphor to convey a biblical understanding of leadership. Good shepherds are deeply committed to the welfare of their flock, just as leaders in God's kingdom must be genuinely concerned for the care and provision of those entrusted to them. True shepherds place the needs of their flock above their own, often at significant personal cost. This role demands that they exercise authority with a balance of tender care and compassion while also possessing the courage and resilience to face and overcome significant challenges.

Shepherd leadership encompasses oversight, protection, provision, care, and guidance of God's people, with human leaders acting as stewards of God's flock. Biblical studies scholar Timothy Laniak eloquently captures this dynamic, writing,

> Our theology of leadership is informed by this breathtaking choice of God to grant royal prerogatives to his creatures. To be made in His image is to rule with Him and for Him. Every shepherd leader is first, and always, a sheep who relates to God as "my Shepherd." This is a dependent relationship on God.[4]

Leaders in the kingdom are appointed by God and empowered by His Spirit, responsible for the flock while remaining accountable to God, the supreme and Great Shepherd of His people. True shepherds serve the flock on behalf of God, never for their own gain or recognition.

THE FAILURE OF SHEPHERD LEADERS: A STUDY OF EZEKIEL 34:1-10

In the book of Ezekiel, the prophet delivers a powerful message of judgment against the shepherd leaders of Israel. These leaders were appointed to care for the people, to protect them from dangers, and to bring back those who had strayed. However, they failed miserably in their responsibilities, prioritizing their own interests over the well-being of the flock. Instead of nurturing and safeguarding the people, they exploited them for personal gain. Ezekiel records this divine indictment:

> The word of the Lord came to me: "Son of man, prophesy against the shepherds of Israel; prophesy, and say to them, even to the shepherds, Thus says the Lord God: Ah, shepherds of Israel who have been feeding yourselves! Should not shepherds feed the sheep? You eat the fat, you clothe yourselves with wool, you slaughter the fat ones, but you do not feed the sheep" (Ezekiel 34:1-3).

Ezekiel continues with a second accusation against these leaders. They neglected the physical and spiritual health of the flock, leaving the sheep vulnerable to predators and danger. The prophet laments:

> The weak you have not strengthened, the sick you have not healed, the injured you have not bound up, the strayed you have not brought back, the lost you have not sought, and with force and harshness you have ruled them. So they were scattered, because there was no shepherd, and they became food for all the wild beasts. My sheep were scattered; they wandered over all the mountains and on every high hill. My sheep were scattered over all the face of the earth, with none to search for them (Ezekiel 34:4-6).

The shepherds of Israel were not only negligent but also abusive, ruling over the people with brutality and indifference. Their irresponsible leadership led to widespread harm and suffering among God's people.

Theologian St. Augustine, reflecting on Ezekiel 34, addresses the issue of shepherds who neglect their flock. He warns,

> You are members of the flock of the Good Shepherd, who watches over Israel and nourishes his people. Yet there are shepherds who want to have the title of shepherd without wanting to fulfill a

pastor's duties; let us then recall what God says to his shepherds through the prophet. You must listen attentively; I must listen with fear and trembling.[5]

God's response to these failed shepherds is severe and uncompromising:

> Therefore, you shepherds, hear the word of the Lord: As I live, declares the Lord God, surely because my sheep have become a prey, and my sheep have become food for all the wild beasts, since there was no shepherd, and because my shepherds have not searched for my sheep, but the shepherds have fed themselves, and have not fed my sheep, therefore, you shepherds, hear the word of the Lord: Thus says the Lord God, Behold, I am against the shepherds, and I will require my sheep at their hand and put a stop to their feeding the sheep. No longer shall the shepherds feed themselves. I will rescue my sheep from their mouths, that they may not be food for them (Ezekiel 34:7-10).

God holds these leaders accountable for their reckless and self-serving actions. They were entrusted with caring for His flock but instead used their positions for personal enrichment. As a result, God declares judgment on them, stripping them of their roles as shepherds and intervening directly to rescue His people.

God is the ultimate Shepherd and the true leader of His people. He assigns undershepherds—leaders who are meant to care for and guide His flock—but these leaders are always accountable to Him. The shepherds judged in Ezekiel's prophecy failed to fulfill their calling, inflicting harm on God's people. In response, God steps in to rescue and restore His scattered flock. He declares through Ezekiel:

> For thus says the Lord God: Behold, I, I myself will search for my sheep and will seek them out. As a shepherd seeks out his flock when he is among his sheep that have been scattered, so will I seek out my sheep, and I will rescue them from all places where they have been scattered on a day of clouds and thick darkness. And I will bring them out from the peoples and gather them from the countries, and will bring them into their own land. And I will feed them on the mountains of Israel, by the ravines, and in all the inhabited places of the country. I will feed them with good pasture, and on the mountain heights of Israel shall be their grazing land. There they shall lie down in good grazing land, and on rich pasture they shall feed on the mountains of Israel. I myself will be the shepherd of my sheep, and I myself will make them lie down, declares the

Lord God. I will seek the lost, and I will bring back the strayed, and I will bind up the injured, and I will strengthen the weak, and the fat and the strong I will destroy. I will feed them in justice (Ezekiel 34:11-16).

In response to the wickedness of Israel's leaders, God promises to gather His scattered people and place them under the leadership of a new shepherd—His servant David. This Davidic leadership is meant to provide lasting security and care for the people of God. As the Lord declares, "And I will set up over them one shepherd, my servant David, and he shall feed them: he shall feed them and be their shepherd. And I, the Lord, will be their God, and my servant David shall be prince among them" (Ezekiel 34:23-24).

GOD'S UNDERSHEPHERDS: THE PROMISE OF FAITHFUL LEADERSHIP

Throughout history, the people of God have suffered under the leadership of selfish and abusive kings, prophets, and priests. In response, God speaks through the prophet Jeremiah to promise a new kind of shepherd—one who would lead sacrificially and with compassion. Jeremiah proclaims, "And I will give you shepherds after my own heart, who will feed you with knowledge and understanding" (Jeremiah 3:15). This promise came at a time of great turmoil and confusion, offering hope of true shepherd leaders who would serve selflessly and reflect God's own heart. This kind of leadership is defined by a commitment to following God and leading as He has modeled. True shepherds lead with a heart characterized by God's love and compassion, coupled with a mind equipped for deep discernment and wisdom.

In the Bible, shepherds served as a metaphor for the rulers of Israel, the leaders of God's people. Jeremiah characterizes the failed leaders of Israel as "stupid shepherds" who did not seek the Lord's guidance, resulting in the scattering of the flock: "For the shepherds are stupid and do not inquire of the Lord; therefore they have not prospered, and all their flock is scattered" (Jeremiah 10:21). The leaders of Israel had fallen short, failing to seek God's wisdom and neglecting the care of His people. In response, God promises to personally tend to His flock and to raise up faithful leaders.

These shepherd leaders, promised by God, will provide a deeper understanding of the people's relationship with Him and lead them toward greater prosperity. As the Lord says in Jeremiah 23:3-4:

> Then I will gather the remnant of my flock out of all the countries where I have driven them, and I will bring them back to their fold, and they shall be fruitful and multiply. I will set shepherds over them who will care for them, and they shall fear no more, nor be dismayed, neither shall any be missing, declares the Lord (Jeremiah 23:3-4).

God is the "Shepherd of shepherds," the ultimate leader who guides His people through the oversight of undershepherds. Throughout the Bible, figures like Moses and David serve as examples of these undershepherds, while Jesus arrives as the divine-human Shepherd of Israel, commissioning His disciples to continue the work of caring for God's people. Empowered by the Holy Spirit, these leaders become God's fellow workers, as the Apostle Paul describes in 1 Corinthians 3:9: "For we are God's fellow workers. You are God's field, God's building." True shepherd leaders serve as God's ambassadors, always taking on a supportive role and prioritizing the well-being of His people.

THE SHEPHERD LEADER: UNDERSTANDING GOD AS THE GREAT SHEPHERD

A shepherd's primary responsibilities are to protect, guide, and feed the flock, ensuring their well-being. Frank Damazio captures the essence of this role, stating, "A shepherd is a man who takes care of the sheep, a person who cares for and protects the sheep; a spiritual guide, friend or companion."[6] The work of a shepherd is both practical and spiritual, serving as an intimate metaphor throughout scripture to describe one who lives closely with the flock and meets their every need—acting as a guide, physician, and protector.

Scripture consistently portrays God as the spiritual Shepherd of His people, providing a perfect example for earthly leaders—undershepherds—to follow. Various passages throughout the Bible identify God as the Great Shepherd, such as:

Psalm 23:1: "The Lord is my shepherd; I shall not want."

Psalm 80:1: "Give ear, O Shepherd of Israel, you who lead Joseph like a flock."

Ezekiel 34:12: "As a shepherd seeks out his flock when he is among his sheep that have been scattered, so will I seek out my sheep, and I will rescue them from all places where they have been scattered on a day of clouds and thick darkness."

Isaiah 40:11: "He will tend his flock like a shepherd; he will gather the lambs in his arms; he will carry them in his bosom, and gently lead those that are with young."

Psalm 77:20: "You led your people like a flock by the hand of Moses and Aaron."

These verses not only establish God as the Great Shepherd but also illustrate the heart attitude and actions that shepherd leaders are called to emulate. The following actions characterize the care God provides as the Great Shepherd:

Ezekiel 34:11-16: Searches out the lost sheep.

Ezekiel 34:12: Rescues the scattered sheep.

Ezekiel 34:13: Gathers the dispersed sheep.

Ezekiel 34:13: Feeds the hungry sheep.

Psalm 23:1-3, Ezekiel 34:15: Rests the weary sheep.

Ezekiel 34:16: Binds up the hurt sheep.

Ezekiel 34:16: Strengthens the weak sheep.

Psalm 23:3: Guides the directionless sheep.

Isaiah 40:11: Carries the sheep.

Psalm 23:3: Restores the soul of the tired sheep.

Psalm 23:4: Comforts the anxious sheep.

Psalm 23:5: Prepares a table for the sheep.

Psalm 23:5: Anoints the sheep.

The imagery of God as a shepherd and His people as sheep is a powerful and recurring theme in the Psalms. For example, Psalm 100:3 declares, "Know that the Lord, he is God! It is he who made us, and we are his; we are his people, and the sheep of his pasture." Psalm 23, written by David, is perhaps the most well-known example of this metaphor. David, who was both a shepherd and the son of a shepherd, later became known as the Shepherd King of Israel. In the opening line of Psalm 23, David boldly proclaims, "The Lord is my shepherd" (Psalm 23:1). Throughout the psalm, David describes an intensely personal relationship with God, highlighting the intimate bond between a shepherd and his sheep. To David, God is not just a distant figure but a close protector and guide. While the metaphor of God as a shepherd is primarily pastoral, it was also used in the ancient Near East to refer to kings and other leaders.

In Psalm 23, David expresses complete trust in the provision, protection, and guidance of God, the Great Shepherd. As a king, David acknowledges his dependence on the divine Shepherd for all his needs. He speaks not as a shepherd himself but as a sheep under the care of the Great Shepherd, modeling a relationship of dependency that all shepherd leaders should emulate. Shepherd leaders in God's kingdom are, first and foremost, sheep who relate to God as "my Shepherd." They are appointed by God and are effective only as they rely on His care and are empowered by His Spirit.

Undershepherds must themselves be shepherded by God to lead and care for His people faithfully. Leaders in God's kingdom require the guidance of the Great Shepherd to walk in His ways. This deep, intimate relationship keeps them from straying as they face the challenges and dangers inherent in life and leadership. Psalm 23 serves as a model for the kind of relationship every shepherd leader needs to maintain with God. Timothy Laniak writes,

> Psalm 23 is a reminder that even the king—especially the king—was dependent on the God of Israel for personal nurture and guidance. Israel's kings had to understand that being a member of the flock of God was more fundamental than being appointed shepherd over that flock.[7]

Shepherd leaders must place their relationship with God above their responsibilities in leading others. Before they can effectively lead God's people, undershepherds must first learn to trust God as their personal, divine Shepherd. This relationship is one of complete dependence, rooted in the understanding that leaders are first and foremost followers. The opening line of Psalm 23 offers shepherd leaders a foundation for a biblically faithful approach to leadership, where the Lord sets the ultimate example of how to guide, mentor, and nurture His people.

David captures this truth in Psalm 23, proclaiming, "The Lord is my shepherd." For leaders in God's kingdom, following the Great Shepherd's methods of guiding, preparing, and caring for those in His care is invaluable. He provides a perfect model of leadership that balances care for others with trust in God's provision. Old Testament scholar Walter Kaiser affirms this point, noting, "God's provision, abundance, and protection will always be there for the shepherd, who is thereby taught to communicate the same to those under his or her leadership."[8]

THE SHEPHERD LEADER: JESUS AS THE GOOD SHEPHERD

The New Testament presents Jesus as the Good Shepherd, revealing Him as the revelation of God in the flesh. Just as God was the shepherd of His people in the Old Testament, Jesus assumes this role in the New Testament, embodying the full expression of the Father's heart on earth. Frank Damazio notes, "Jesus was the full expression of the heart of the heavenly Father on earth. His words, His ways, and His actions all manifested the heart of the Father."[9] This truth is affirmed in John 10:30, where Jesus declares that He and the Father are one—united in mind, purpose, and action. Jesus further emphasizes this oneness in John 14:9, saying, "Whoever has seen me has seen the Father." The mutual indwelling between the Father and the Son means that Jesus' words and works are direct reflections of the Father's will. Jesus explained this truth to His disciples in John 8:28-29:

> When you have lifted up the Son of Man, then you will know that I am he, and that I do nothing on my own authority, but speak just as the Father taught me. And he who sent me is with me. He has not left me alone, for I always do the things that are pleasing to him.

The following scriptures identify Jesus as the Good Shepherd in the New Testament:

John 10:11, 14: "I am the Good Shepherd."

Hebrews 13:20: "Jesus, the Great Shepherd of the sheep."

1 Peter 2:25: "For you were straying like sheep, but have now returned to the Shepherd and Overseer of your souls."

1 Peter 5:4: "When the Chief Shepherd appears."

Jesus exemplified the heart and actions of a true shepherd throughout His life and ministry. His shepherding was driven by love and compassion, always focused on meeting the needs of the sheep. A key aspect of His role as the Good Shepherd was His willingness to lay down His life for the flock. The following actions demonstrate the care that the Good Shepherd provides:

Matthew 9:35-36; John 10:15: Cares for the sheep.

John 10:3: Relates to the sheep.

John 10:1: Condemns all who reject the Door of the sheepfold and enter some other way, as thieves and robbers.

John 10:8: Condemns all who came before Him as thieves and robbers.

John 10:1: Provides a sheepfold for the sheep.

John 10:3-4: Leads the sheep.

John 10:2: Enters by the Door Himself.

John 10:3: Has the doorkeeper open to Him.

John 10:6: Provides spiritual insight for the sheep.

John 10:3, 27: Makes His voice plain to His sheep.

John 10:3: Calls His own sheep by name.

John 10:3: Leads His own sheep out into pasture.

John 10:4: Goes before His own sheep as He leads them out.

John 10:4, 27: Has the sheep follow Him.

John 10:4: Has the sheep recognize His voice.

John 10:7, 9: Is the Door of the sheep.

John 10:9: Feeds the sheep.

John 10:10: Gives life to the sheep by protecting them.

John 10:10, 11, 15, 17: Gives His life for the sheep.

John 10:11, 14: Is the Good Shepherd of the sheep.

John 10:12-13: Is a true Shepherd of His sheep and the opposite of a hireling.

John 10:12: Is the owner of the sheep and not a hireling.

John 10:12: Sees when the wolf comes to destroy the flock.

John 10:12: Stays near the sheep when the wolf comes, in contrast to the cowardly hireling.

John 10:14, 27: Knows His own sheep.

John 10:14: Is known by His own sheep.

John 10:15: Knows the Father.

John 10:15: Is known by the Father.

John 10:16: Has other sheep in other folds.

John 10:16: Brings in the other sheep also.

John 10:16: Is heard by the other sheep as well.

John 10:16: Is the One Shepherd and owner of all folds.

John 10:17: Takes up His life again because He laid it down.

John 10:18: Lays His life down freely and by His own initiative.

John 10:18: Has the authority to lay down His life because God Himself has commissioned Him to do so.

God had long promised to send a faithful shepherd to care for His people, as foretold by the prophet Ezekiel. God declared through Ezekiel, "And I will set up over them one shepherd, my servant David, and he shall feed them: he shall feed them and be their shepherd" (Ezekiel 32:23). This reference to David is not about the historical figure but points to the Messianic Shepherd—Jesus. God established Jesus as the chosen Good Shepherd, entrusting Him with the care of His people. Jesus affirmed this role, declaring in John 10:11, "I am the good shepherd. The good shepherd lays down his life for the sheep," and reiterating in verses 14-15, "I am the good shepherd. I know my own and my own know me, just as the Father knows me and I know the Father; and I lay down my life for the sheep." As the Good Shepherd, Jesus is the true

King of Israel and the obedient Servant of God, embodying the character and actions of a true shepherd.

Shepherd leadership, as modeled by Jesus, requires great sacrifice for the well-being of the sheep. The ultimate example of this sacrifice was demonstrated at Calvary, where Jesus, the perfect Good Shepherd, gave His life for God's flock. Phillip Keller reflects on this truth, writing,

> The blood shed for the sheep is what makes them precious to the Good Shepherd. Likewise, the cost and sacrifice that an undershepherd pays for his sheep makes them precious to him. Sheep require endless attention and meticulous care. The shepherd must continually lay down his life for them if they were to flourish and prosper.[10]

Jesus demonstrated that no sacrifice is too great for the well-being of the sheep. He willingly obeyed the Father, even to the point of laying down His life for the sake of those He led. A true shepherd leader exemplifies deep love for the sheep, fully embracing the role of their shepherd, and is willing to endure immense pain and difficulty to ensure their protection and care. Shepherd leadership must be marked by the same self-sacrificial leadership that Jesus displayed.

The Old Testament prophets spoke out against the false shepherds who mistreated and abandoned God's people, underscoring the urgent need for true, faithful leaders. In Ezekiel 34:23, God promised to send a Shepherd who would save Israel—a promise the gospels present as fulfilled in Jesus. One of the most profound depictions of Jesus as the Good Shepherd appears in John 10:1-21, where two essential themes emerge. First, Jesus is portrayed as the Good Shepherd who willingly lays down His life for His sheep. Second, Jesus provides the ultimate model of leadership for those who serve as undershepherds. John emphasizes that the heart motivation of a shepherd is more crucial than the practical aspects of leadership—Jesus embodies genuine concern for the welfare of the sheep above all else.

The Good Shepherd discourse in John 10 serves as a leadership model for those called to be shepherd leaders. Jesus presented this example to instruct His undershepherds on how to care for God's people faithfully. In this passage, Jesus emphasizes the sacrificial nature of true leadership, contrasting the Good Shepherd, who lays down His life for the sheep, with the hired hand, who abandons the flock in the face of danger. He declares, "I am the door. If anyone enters by me, he will be saved and will go in and out and find pasture. The thief comes only to steal and kill and destroy. I came that they may have life and have it abundantly. I am the good shepherd. The good shepherd lays down his life for the sheep" (John 10:9–11).

This teaching underscores the call to selfless service, intimate relationship, and unwavering commitment required of shepherd leaders. Just as the sheep recognize the voice of their shepherd and follow him, faithful leaders are to lead with integrity and love, guiding others toward abundant life in

Christ. Through this example, they reflect the ultimate care of the Good Shepherd who knows His own, calls them by name, and leads them to safety and flourishing.

Building on the example of the Good Shepherd, Jesus not only modeled sacrificial leadership but also actively prepared His disciples to carry on His mission. He equipped them with the authority, guidance, and responsibility to emulate His care and commitment in their own roles as shepherd leaders. The following scriptures demonstrate how Jesus instructed and empowered His disciples to reflect His example in their leadership and ministry.

John 14:12: "Truly, truly, I say to you, whoever believes in me will also do the works that I do; and greater works than these will he do, because I am going to the Father."

John 20:21-23: Jesus said to them again, "Peace be with you. As the Father has sent me, even so I am sending you." And when he had said this, he breathed on them and said to them, "Receive the Holy Spirit. If you forgive the sins of any, they are forgiven them; if you withhold forgiveness from any, it is withheld."

John 21:15-19: When they had finished breakfast, Jesus said to Simon Peter, "Simon, son of John, do you love me more than these?" He said to him, "Yes, Lord; you know that I love you." He said to him, "Feed my lambs." He said to him a second time, "Simon, son of John, do you love me?" He said to him, "Yes, Lord; you know that I love you." He said to him, "Tend my sheep." He said to him the third time, "Do you love me?" and he said to him, "Lord, you know everything; you know that I love you." Jesus said to him, "Feed my sheep. Truly, truly, I say to you, when you were young, you used to dress yourself and walk wherever you wanted, but when you are old, you will stretch out your hands, and another will dress you and carry you where you do not want to go." (This he said to show by what kind of death he was to glorify God.) And after saying this he said to him, "Follow me."

Jesus sent His disciples to feed His sheep, preparing them to emulate His life and ministry as the Good Shepherd. However, this responsibility does not grant them the authority to rule over the flock. Instead, undershepherds are entrusted with the task of guiding and caring for the sheep, with a role defined by love rather than power. Their leadership should reflect a deep commitment to the well-being of the flock, embodying the self-sacrificial love that Jesus demonstrated.

In 1 Peter 5:1-4, Peter provides an instructive word to shepherd leaders, urging them to:

Shepherd the flock of God that is among you, exercising oversight, not under compulsion, but willingly, as God would have you; not for shameful gain, but eagerly; not domineering over those in your charge, but being examples to the flock. And when the chief Shepherd appears, you will receive the unfading crown of glory.

The Good Shepherd is "good" because He loves and treasures the sheep, willingly sacrificing His own life for their benefit. Likewise, the leadership of undershepherds must be characterized by the same love and devotion. The sheep belong to God, and shepherd leaders will ultimately be accountable to Him for how they care for His flock.

THE PURPOSE AND MOTIVES OF THE MINISTRY LEADER

Jesus serves as the ultimate example of the heart attitude that a true shepherd should have toward God's people. His care for them was driven by profound love and compassion, even to the point of laying down His life. True shepherd leaders, therefore, are marked by this same sacrificial love for the flock, modeling the standard that Jesus set. The relationship between a shepherd leader and the sheep should be rooted in unconditional love and genuine concern, not dependent on the actions or attitudes of the flock. More importantly, the love a shepherd leader expresses toward God's people is a response to the love they have received from the Lord. This concept is powerfully conveyed in 1 John 4:7-11:

> Beloved, let us love one another, for love is from God, and whoever loves has been born of God and knows God. Anyone who does not love does not know God, because God is love. In this the love of God was made manifest among us, that God sent his only Son into the world, so that we might live through him. In this is love, not that we have loved God but that he loved us and sent his Son to be the propitiation for our sins. Beloved, if God so loved us, we also ought to love one another.

For shepherd leaders, cultivating and maintaining a close and intimate relationship with the Good Shepherd is essential. This deep connection enables them to hear His voice clearly and to mirror His heart, allowing them to be driven by love in their care for God's people.

In His synagogue sermon, as recorded in the Gospel of Luke, Jesus revealed the guiding motives for all shepherd leaders:

> The Spirit of the Lord is upon Me, because He has anointed Me to preach the gospel to the poor; He has sent Me to heal the brokenhearted, to proclaim liberty to the captives and recovery of sight to the

blind, to set at liberty those who are oppressed; to proclaim the acceptable year of the Lord (Luke 4:18-19, NKJV).

In this passage, Jesus fulfills the prophetic words of Isaiah 61, declaring the purpose of His mission. The kingdom of God had arrived, and Jesus was actively bringing it to fruition. His mission included preaching the good news of the kingdom to the poor and imprisoned, healing the brokenhearted, restoring sight to the blind, and offering relief and forgiveness to the persecuted.

Jesus understood that the core purpose of His ministry was to bring the good news of the kingdom to those who were distressed and suffering. Through His teachings, God broke the power of sin, established communion with the Father, and enabled His will to be fulfilled.

God anointed Jesus through the Spirit to accomplish His work; every aspect of Jesus' life and ministry was marked by the Holy Spirit's presence and power as He fulfilled God's eternal purposes. Jesus commissions shepherd leaders to continue this mission and ministry, empowering them with the same Spirit. This sacred assignment is fulfilled by embodying Jesus' purpose and motives in ministry, ensuring that the work of the Good Shepherd continues through those who lead His people.

SHEPHERD LEADERSHIP: EMBODYING THE HEART OF THE GOOD SHEPHERD

Paul Tripp offers profound insight for pastors and church leaders, stating, "Pastoral ministry is always shaped by a war between the kingdom of self and the kingdom of God, which is fought on the field of your heart."[11] Jesus exemplifies a life lived for the glory of God rather than for personal gain, showing His followers how to live beyond selfish ambitions. The Apostle Paul echoes this call, urging, "And he died for all, that those who live might no longer live for themselves but for him who for their sake died and was raised" (2 Corinthians 5:15).

Church leaders face a crucial choice: to serve either the kingdom of self or the kingdom of God. This decision reveals the true ruler of their hearts. Jesus provided the clear answer when He taught, "Your kingdom come, your will be done, on earth as it is in heaven" (Matthew 6:10). True shepherd leaders follow Jesus, the Good Shepherd, by embodying the heart of the Father in their guidance, protection, and provision for God's people. They demonstrate kingdom leadership through sacrifice and selflessness, living for the glory of God alone.

The model of shepherd leadership, as revealed in scripture and embodied by Jesus, provides a powerful and transformative guide for kingdom leadership. Shepherd leaders are called to serve others with humility, compassion, and an unwavering commitment to the well-being of those entrusted to their care. Just as Jesus, the Good Shepherd, laid down His life for the flock, leaders in God's kingdom must prioritize the needs of others above their own, embodying the heart of the Father.

This chapter emphasizes the essential qualities required for shepherd leadership: servanthood, sacrifice, and a deep reliance on God. Leaders must first recognize that they are followers—sheep who must be led by the Great Shepherd before they can effectively shepherd others. Their mission is not self-promotion but the faithful advancement of God's kingdom, achieved through the careful stewardship of His people.

Reflecting on the failures of Israel's shepherds in Ezekiel 34 and the promise of faithful leadership fulfilled through Christ, the importance of true shepherd leadership becomes evident. Such leaders must be motivated by love and driven by the self-sacrificial nature that Jesus exemplified throughout His life and ministry. This model of leadership redefines authority and power, calling leaders to a life of service that honors God and promotes the spiritual health of His people. Ultimately, the true measure of successful kingdom leadership lies in how closely it mirrors the heart of the Good Shepherd, guiding and caring for others with integrity, compassion, and a deep commitment to glorifying God.

Chapter Eight

FOUNDATIONAL CHARACTERISTICS OF KINGDOM LEADERSHIP

KINGDOM LEADERSHIP: EMBRACING GOSPEL-CENTERED PRINCIPLES IN MINISTRY

THE KINGDOM of God was not only the central priority for Jesus but also the driving motivation and core purpose of His mission and ministry. He declared, "I must preach the good news of the kingdom of God to the other towns as well; for I was sent for this purpose" (Luke 4:43). The kingdom of God defined every aspect of Jesus' life and ministry. After His resurrection, He dedicated forty days to teaching His disciples about the kingdom. Luke records, "He presented himself alive to them after his suffering by many proofs, appearing to them during forty days and speaking about the kingdom of God" (Acts 1:3).

For Jesus, the kingdom of God was of utmost importance, and He emphasized its significance to the disciples, instructing them to make it their highest pursuit. He urged them, "But seek first the kingdom of God and his righteousness, and all these things will be added to you" (Matthew 6:33). Through this command, Jesus conveyed that the kingdom of God was the essential foundation upon which they could build everything else in life. This message served as a crucial reminder for the disciples to prioritize the eternal principles and values of the kingdom over the temporary and fleeting concerns of the world.

Leadership in the kingdom of God stands in stark contrast to worldly concepts of power and influence. Kingdom leaders are not defined by the values of this world but serve as representatives and ambassadors of Jesus, guiding others toward God's kingdom. Robert Stacy captures this idea, stating,

> Leaders, therefore, are living, breathing intimations of the kingdom, foreshadowing in this world the vision and values of that world. They are "kingdom guides," and as such express "leadership" appropriate to the new reality in which they live.[1]

Kingdom leaders should embody the principles that Jesus lived by, with their character and behavior reflecting kingdom values. Leadership under God's reign demands a distinct and unwavering commitment to Christ and the mission of the kingdom, standing firm against the pressures to conform to worldly standards.

True kingdom leadership is distinct and countercultural, marked by an uncompromising devotion to Christ and the mission of the kingdom. Yet, many ministry leaders are swayed by cultural trends and corporate principles, prioritizing secular leadership models above the values of God's kingdom. This misalignment leads to a significant issue: attempting to carry out God's work according to worldly standards. Paul Tripp addresses this concern, asking,

> Could it be that we are looking to the wrong models to understand how to lead? Could it be that as we have become enamored with corporate models of leadership, we have lost sight of deeper gospel insights and values?

He adds, "I am convinced from conversation after conversation with pastors and their leadership that we have a leadership crisis."[2]

The challenge for kingdom leaders is to reject the influence of secular principles and ground their leadership in the timeless truths of God's kingdom. By doing so, they can embody the countercultural values of Jesus and effectively guide others in alignment with God's mission.

A CALL TO GOSPEL-DRIVEN LEADERSHIP

Kingdom leadership is not merely about holding a title or position; it is a high calling marked by a deep commitment to embody the gospel of Jesus Christ in every facet of life and leadership. The foundation of this leadership is the gospel itself, serving not only as a message of salvation but as a comprehensive guide for how followers of Christ should live, think, and act—especially those called to lead.

Kingdom leadership stands in sharp contrast to worldly leadership, prioritizing the advancement of God's purposes over self-promotion or personal success. It centers on the leader's responsibility to live out gospel principles with integrity, service, and selflessness.

This chapter explores the foundational characteristics essential for effective leadership in God's kingdom. It begins by examining the leader's commitment to God's purposes, grounded in the gospel, which shapes and guides their leadership practices. It also considers how Jesus exemplified this commitment, modeling a life of obedience to the Father's will and calling all leaders to follow His example.

Through the lens of Jesus' life and ministry, this chapter addresses the cost of leadership, emphasizing the demands of humility, self-denial, and a commitment to gospel-centered principles. Ministry leaders are called not only to guide others but to lead with a heart of servanthood and sacrifice, reflecting Christ's own approach. The chapter further highlights Spirit-empowered leadership, accountability, and love as essential elements of effective ministry. Ultimately, kingdom leadership involves aligning one's life and work with God's purposes, with Christ as the perfect model and guide for every leader.

COMMITMENT TO GOD'S AGENDA: THE GOSPEL IS THE STANDARD

The Gospel of Jesus Christ is not just a message of salvation; it serves as a comprehensive guide for how followers of Christ should live, think, and act in the world. It lays out a system of values that shapes the behavior and mindset of Christians, particularly those called to leadership within the kingdom of God. The Apostle Paul, in his letter to the Ephesians, underscores this principle by urging believers to "walk in a manner worthy of the calling to which you have been called, with all humility and gentleness, with patience, bearing with one another in love, eager to maintain the unity of the Spirit in the bond of peace" (Ephesians 4:1-3). Paul reminded the Ephesians of the gospel truths meant to shape their thinking and interactions with one another. He introduced a new standard of behavior expected of God's people. This standard calls them to live in a way that is countercultural and distinct from the norms of secular society. Leaders in God's kingdom are called to embrace and embody these gospel characteristics, ensuring that their leadership is both grounded in and guided by its principles.

For leaders in God's kingdom, embodying and upholding the values of the gospel is not merely important—it is indispensable. Their leadership must be deeply anchored in and consistently shaped by the core truths of the gospel. As Paul Tripp insightfully observes,

> The model for the community that is the church, and most importantly its leadership, is the gospel of Jesus Christ. Now, I know that this seems both obvious and vague, but I am persuaded that it is neither, and that if the primary driving force of leadership in local churches around the world was the gospel of Jesus Christ, many of the sad things we have seen happen in the lives of leaders and their churches would not have happened.[3]

The gospel should function as the essential blueprint that directs how leaders approach and carry out their responsibilities within the church. It provides everything necessary for kingdom leaders to find encouragement, strength, and empowerment for their ministry. When leadership is firmly rooted in biblical wisdom and aligned with the authority bestowed by Jesus, ministry leaders are positioned to lead with faithfulness and produce lasting, fruitful outcomes in their service to God's people.

Leadership within God's kingdom carries a tremendous responsibility, one that requires discerning God's will and pursuing His purposes with complete devotion, under the guidance and empowerment of the Holy Spirit. Kingdom leaders must be unwavering in their commitment to lead according to God's way and to align their leadership with His divine agenda. Their leadership principles should be firmly rooted in biblical truth, with scripture serving as the ultimate measure of their leadership.

The book of James offers a sobering reminder of the seriousness of this calling, warning, "Not many of you should become teachers, my brothers, for you know that we who teach will be judged with greater strictness" (James 3:1). Luke similarly highlights the gravity of leadership, stating, "Everyone to whom much was given, of him much will be required, and from him to whom they entrusted much, they will demand the more" (Luke 12:48). Scripture sets high, uncompromising standards for those who serve as ambassadors of Christ, emphasizing the significant personal accountability required of those entrusted with leading God's people.

COMMITMENT TO GOD'S AGENDA: JESUS IS THE MODEL

Jesus exemplified kingdom leadership through His unwavering commitment to the Father's agenda, consistently prioritizing God's will and fulfilling His divine purposes. A defining trait of Jesus' leadership was His deep dependence on His relationship with the Father. He was continually attuned to the Father's voice, allowing Him to discern God's will and remain focused on it without distraction. He declared, "Truly, truly, I say to you, the Son can do nothing of his own accord, but only what he sees the Father doing. For whatever the Father does, that the Son does likewise" (John 5:19). In His complete submission to the Father, Jesus consistently sought to please Him, never acting apart from the Father's direction. Theologian Donald Carson aptly explains,

> The Father initiates, sends, commands, commissions, grants; the Son responds, obeys, performs his Father's will, receives authority. In this sense, the Son is the Father's agent...though much more than an agent.[4]

In this way, Jesus set the ultimate standard for leadership within God's kingdom, offering a powerful model for ministry leaders to follow as they align themselves with God's agenda. Christ-centered leaders are called to cultivate an intimate relationship with the Father, ensuring their actions are rooted in His will and devoted to building the kingdom of God. Every ministry leader's deepest desire should mirror Jesus' own prayer: "Your kingdom come, your will be done, on earth as it is in heaven" (Matthew 6:10).

THE COST OF LEADERSHIP: SERVANTHOOD AND HUMILITY

Leadership within the kingdom of God comes with a profound cost, intensifying the inherent sufferings and challenges of life. Kingdom leaders must be prepared to pay this price, which includes self-sacrifice, loneliness, fatigue, criticism, rejection, and immense pressure. Harold Myra and Marshall Shelley, authors of *The Leadership Secrets of Billy Graham*, describe leadership as being "forged in the furnace...a set of life experiences melded by intense heat."[5] Billy Graham deeply understood this weight, fully aware of the cost that comes with a life completely surrendered to God. Sherwood Wirt, editor of Graham's *Decision* magazine, aptly noted, "All attempts to explain Billy Graham fail unless they begin at the cross."[6] Graham embraced the intense pressures of his calling, allowing them to refine, purify, and empower him throughout his life and ministry. He never shied away from the heat of the furnace, using it to shape himself into a faithful and passionate leader for the kingdom.

The Apostle Paul also recognized the immense pressures of ministry leadership, experiencing loneliness, depression, and discouragement while serving God. His hardships are well-documented in scripture:

Are they servants of Christ? I am a better one—I am talking like a madman—with far greater labors, far more imprisonments, with countless beatings, and often near death. Five times I received at the hands of the Jews the forty lashes less one. Three times I was beaten with rods. Once I was stoned. Three times I was shipwrecked; a night and a day I was adrift at sea; on frequent journeys, in danger from rivers, danger from robbers, danger from my own people, danger from Gentiles, danger in the city, danger in the wilderness, danger at sea, danger from false brothers; in toil and hardship, through many a sleepless night, in hunger and thirst, often without food, in cold and exposure. And apart from other things, there is the daily pressure on me of my anxiety for all the churches" (2 Corinthians 11:23-28).

Paul's trials—imprisonment, beatings, near-death experiences, and constant dangers—illustrate the extreme and unrelenting tension of his life in service to Christ. Yet, he embraced this life wholeheartedly, declaring, "For I decided to know nothing among you except Jesus Christ and him crucified" (1 Corinthians 2:2). Christ crucified was the guiding purpose of Paul's life and ministry.

Answering the call to leadership within the church means embracing a life of sacrifice, self-denial, and suffering. Paul Tripp aptly states, "There simply is no such thing as a call to ministry leadership that isn't also a call to a life of servanthood, and there is no such thing as a call to servanthood that isn't also a call to suffer."[7] This lesson was difficult for the disciples to grasp, as demonstrated by their arguments over who was the greatest:

They went on from there and passed through Galilee. And he did not want anyone to know, for he was teaching his disciples, saying to them, "The

Son of Man is going to be delivered into the hands of men, and they will kill him. And when he is killed, after three days he will rise." But they did not understand the saying, and were afraid to ask him. And they came to Capernaum. And when he was in the house he asked them, "What were you discussing on the way?" But they kept silent, for on the way they had argued with one another about who was the greatest. And he sat down and called the twelve. And he said to them, "If anyone would be first, he must be last of all and servant of all." And he took a child and put him in the midst of them, and taking him in his arms, he said to them, "Whoever receives one such child in my name receives me, and whoever receives me, receives not me but him who sent me" (Mark 9:30-37).

The disciples were preoccupied with their own status, unable to comprehend the suffering and death Jesus was about to endure. Jesus taught them that true greatness in the kingdom of God comes through servanthood. Kingdom leadership is not marked by power and position but by a heart of sacrifice and service. Another instance of the disciples' misguided thinking is highlighted in the following passage:

And James and John, the sons of Zebedee, came up to him and said to him, "Teacher, we want you to do for us whatever we ask of you." And he said to them, "What do you want me to do for you?" And they said to him, "Grant us to sit, one at your right hand and one at your left, in your glory." Jesus said to them, "You do not know what you are asking. Are you able to drink the cup that I drink, or to be baptized with the baptism with which I am baptized?" And they said to him, "We are able." And Jesus said to them, "The cup that I drink you will drink, and with the baptism with which I am baptized, you will be baptized, but to sit at my right hand or at my left is not mine to grant, but it is for those for whom it has been prepared." And when the ten heard it, they began to be indignant at James and John. And Jesus called them to him and said to them, "You know that those who are considered rulers of the Gentiles lord it over them, and their great ones exercise authority over them. But it shall not be so among you. But whoever would be great among you must be your servant, and whoever would be first among you must be slave of all. For even the Son of Man came not to be served but to serve, and to give his life as a ransom for many" (Mark 10:35-45).

James and John, preoccupied with rank and superiority, missed Jesus' teaching on suffering. Instead of focusing on His message, they became consumed with self-interest, seeking status, power, and authority over others. Jesus responded by reminding them that leadership in His kingdom is not about lording power over others but about serving and sacrificing for them. Though Jesus was rightfully entitled to a life of power, position, and authority, He willingly chose a path of service and sacrifice, humbling Himself to the point of taking on the role of a servant, even unto death.

Leadership in God's kingdom is a weighty responsibility that requires significant sacrifice, beginning at the cross. Jesus clarified this expectation to His disciples, saying, "If anyone would come after me, let him deny himself and take up his cross and follow me. For whoever would save his life will lose it, but whoever loses his life for my sake will find it" (Matthew 6:24-25). Jesus fully embodied suffering, self-denial, and the cross throughout His life. The cross is not only central to Jesus' life but to the lives of all who follow Him. Robert Stacy emphasizes, "There is no path to the kingdom of God that bypasses the cross. The cross is not merely the consequence of being a disciple; it is constitutive to it."[8] Kingdom leadership demands the surrender of personal control and the complete acceptance of God's sovereignty. This cruciform approach is fundamental for every follower of Christ. Self-denial is not optional for those who seek to follow Christ and lead in His kingdom.

Kingdom leaders must model servant leadership by prioritizing the well-being of those they lead. This leadership is characterized by humility, self-denial, and a willingness to suffer for the sake of the kingdom—traits at the heart of the gospel and embodied by Jesus. Leaders in God's kingdom must adopt the cruciform way of the cross, rejecting the pursuit of popularity, success, and greatness while embracing suffering and failure. Jack Hayford, renowned pastor and author, insightfully stated:

> True leadership is found only at *Jesus' feet* and is shaped and kept only *in the heart*. Fruitful leadership is not the capacity to "produce results" but the "capacity to bring those I lead to their deepest enrichment and highest fulfillment." Fruitful leadership is not getting others to fulfill my goals (or even my God-given vision for our collective enterprise and good), but helping others realize God's creative intent for their lives.[9]

Jesus consistently condemned actions driven by a desire for approval and affection from others, expecting His disciples to reject all actions motivated by selfish ambition and personal gain. Their identity and contentment were to be found entirely in God. The lessons Jesus taught His disciples remain guiding principles for today's church leaders. Pastor and author Peter Scazzero writes,

The pathway Jesus calls us to walk is an intentional move away from greatness-ism to being little or lowly. Jesus said, "Whoever takes the lowly position of this child is the greatest in the kingdom of heaven" (Matthew 18:4).[10]

A biblical understanding of servanthood is grounded in Jesus' example. He led by embracing love and rejecting the pursuit of power. Servant leaders must be driven by humility, not ego. Power, control, and the pursuit of platform and position are not priorities for those who follow Christ. Instead, they seek God's will and serve others with love. Walter C. Wright, executive director of the Max De Pree Center for Leadership, explains, "The greatest ones in the kingdom of God will be the servants, those who invest their lives in the people around them, not from positions of leadership, but in relationships of service."[11]

SPIRIT-EMPOWERED LEADERSHIP: SPIRITUAL WARFARE

Ministry leadership is spiritual warfare, placing those in positions of authority on the front lines of spiritual attack. Paul Tripp emphasizes, "Leadership in the church of Jesus Christ is not just a battle for theological faithfulness, gospel purity, and methodological integrity; it is also always a war for the heart of every leader."[12] The very nature of ministry makes it a prime target for the enemy's attacks, as it is through ministry that the enemy seeks to undermine and defeat leaders. Tripp further warns, "Leaders unaware of the spiritual war that is ministry begin to minister with kidnapped hearts, distorted vision, and misguided motivations."[13]

Scripture consistently warns about the ongoing reality of spiritual warfare, urging leaders to remain vigilant and aware of the daily spiritual battles they face. The Apostle Paul issued a clear and urgent warning to the early church regarding these unseen battles, stating,

> For we do not wrestle against flesh and blood, but against the rulers, against the authorities, against the cosmic powers over this present darkness, against the spiritual forces of evil in the heavenly places (Ephesians 6:12).

Paul's intent was to expose the cunning and immense power of these dark spiritual forces, equipping the church to stand firm and overcome them. These spiritual adversaries operate in secrecy, working in the shadows where Satan deploys them to sow destruction, chaos, and wickedness.

John Stott offers further insight, noting that the devil rarely attacks openly but prefers to operate in darkness. He explains,

> The devil seldom attacks openly, preferring darkness to light, that when he transforms himself into "an angel of light" we are caught unsuspecting. He

is a dangerous wolf, but enters Christ's flock in the disguise of a sheep. Sometimes he roars like a lion, but more often is as subtle as a serpent. We must not imagine, therefore, that open persecution and open temptation to sin are his only or even his commonest weapons; he prefers to seduce us into compromise and deceive us into error.[14]

In light of this spiritual battlefield, ministry leaders must remain constantly aware of the threats that surround them. They must take intentional steps to avoid behaviors that expose them to demonic attacks. Tripp underscores the risk, stating,

Pride in ministry achievements puts you in battle danger. Lack of openness to the pastoral care and concern of fellow leaders exposes you to danger. Surrounding yourself with leaders who are no longer willing or are too fearful to challenge and confront you is to leave yourself exposed.[15]

Spiritual warfare is not an afterthought but a central reality for those in ministry leadership. Leaders must be fully equipped, ready to dismantle spiritual strongholds and resist the enemy's attacks with resilience and discernment.

SPIRIT-EMPOWERED LEADERSHIP: SPIRIT EMPOWERMENT

In his article "Power and Authority in Pentecostal Leadership," John F. Carter asserts that "the exercise of leadership is ultimately an exercise in power."[16] Leadership, by its very nature, involves exercising authority over others, with human power often driven by personal effort and charisma. However, divine power transcends these limitations, being supernaturally manifested through the Holy Spirit. When leadership is infused with the Spirit's power, it rises above mere human effort, becoming truly Spirit-empowered leadership.

Jesus is the perfect model for this kind of leadership, demonstrating both power (*dynamis*) and authority (*exousia*) throughout His ministry. The Gospel of Luke illustrates, "And they were all amazed and said to one another, 'What is this word? For with authority and power he commands the unclean spirits, and they come out!'" (Luke 4:36). Jesus Himself affirms His divine authority: "And Jesus came and said to them, 'All authority in heaven and on earth has been given to me'" (Matthew 28:18). Biblical scholar James Shelton observes, "Jesus is the Spirit-led man *par* excellence."[17] He exercised supernatural power and authority through the Holy Spirit, setting a model of Spirit-empowered leadership for His followers to emulate.

The final commission that Jesus gave to His disciples before His ascension is found in the book of Acts. His commission demonstrates the critical role that the Holy Spirit fulfills in empowering followers of Jesus to continue

His ministry. Jesus declared, "But you will receive power when the Holy Spirit has come upon you, and you will be my witnesses in Jerusalem and in all Judea and Samaria, and to the end of the earth" (Acts 1:8).

DEPENDENCE ON GOD

Billy Graham understood that his spiritual power and effectiveness as a ministry leader were firmly rooted in his dependence on God. His life and ministry were characterized by a deep commitment to prayer and spending time in God's presence. Cliff Barrows described Graham with these words:

> He was confident in God. He sought God's will, he was God-dependent, motivated by his love for God and man. He was self-effacing, but he was secure in the place of God's appointment. He was anointed of God. He was considerate. He was not authoritarian.[18]

Like Graham, David also exemplified profound trust in God's presence and power. He confidently declared, "The Lord who delivered me from the paw of the lion and from the paw of the bear will deliver me from the hand of this Philistine" (1 Samuel 17:37). David's complete reliance on God is further reflected in the Psalms, where he wrote,

For God alone, O my soul, wait in silence, for my hope is from him. He only is my rock and my salvation, my fortress; I shall not be shaken. On God rests my salvation and my glory; my mighty rock, my refuge is God (Psalm 62:5-7).

For ministry leaders, dwelling in God's presence is essential for being equipped, empowered, and guided in their work. It is in His presence that leaders find their source of hope, confidence, motivation, and refuge.

Silence and stillness in God's presence are critical for nurturing a leader's relationship with Him, strengthening them for the demands of ministry. Ministry leaders must prioritize withdrawing from the pressures of their roles to allow God to renew and refill them. Solitude invites leaders to pray and abide in God's presence, creating space for spiritual transformation. Peter Scazzero highlights this truth, saying, "Integrating silence and stillness utterly transforms the way we follow Jesus and the way we lead."[19]

Solitude allows ministry leaders to surrender their ambitions and align themselves with the Father's will. In these quiet moments, God performs the deep, transformative work needed for their spiritual and emotional well-being, free from the distractions of the outside world. It is in this sacred space that God ministers directly to the leader, creating a powerful opportunity for a life-changing encounter with Him. Ruth Haley Barton describes this process of transformation as one where, the Spirit of God moves us from behaviors motivated by fear and self-protection to trust and abandonment to God; from selfishness and self-absorption to freely offering the gifts of the authentic self; from the ego's desperate attempts to control the outcomes of our lives to an ability to give ourselves over to the will of God which is often the foolishness of this world.[20]

In solitude, leaders can surrender their ambitions to God's will, allowing Him to perform the transformative work necessary for their spiritual and emotional health.

Seeking God and spending time in His presence are crucial practices for ministry leaders. Transformative encounters with God in solitude nourish and strengthen the leader's soul, enabling them to guide others toward those same encounters. Henri Nouwen reminds leaders,

We are responsible for our own solitude. Without such a desert, we will lose our own soul while preaching the gospel to others. But with such a spiritual abode, we will become increasingly conformed to him in whose Name we minister.[21]

Jesus modeled a life that prioritized time in God's presence because He understood that dependence on the Father was vital for His life and ministry. His life was characterized by solitude and prayer, disciplines that the disciples witnessed firsthand. Jesus prayed constantly, often retreating to solitary places in the early morning or late at night to commune with the Father. The Gospels provide numerous examples of Jesus' dedication to prayer:

And after he had dismissed the crowds, he went up on the mountain by himself to pray (Matthew 14:23).

And after he had taken leave of them, he went up on the mountain to pray (Mark 6:46).

In these days he went out to the mountain to pray, and all night he continued in prayer to God (Luke 6:12).

And rising very early in the morning, while it was still dark, he departed and went out to a desolate place, and there he prayed (Mark 1:35).

But he would withdraw to desolate places and pray (Luke 5:16).

Now Jesus was praying in a certain place, and when he finished, one of his disciples said to him, "Lord, teach us to pray, as John taught his disciples" (Luke 11:1).

Through prayer, God transforms individuals, aligning their thoughts, desires, and affections with His own. Richard Foster underscores the centrality of prayer in the spiritual life, saying, "Of all the Spiritual Disciplines prayer is the most central because it ushers us into perpetual communion with the Father."[22] This ongoing communion with God is essential for becoming more conformed to the image of Christ through the power of the Holy Spirit.

The Apostle Paul frequently emphasized the necessity of prayer, recognizing its power and importance. His letters reveal his deep commitment to this practice:

Pray without ceasing, give thanks in all circumstances; for this is the will of God in Christ Jesus for you (1 Thessalonians 5:17-18).

Rejoice in hope, be patient in tribulation, be constant in prayer (Romans 12:12).

Praying at all times in the Spirit, with all prayer and supplication. To that end, keep alert with all perseverance, making supplication for all the saints, and also for me, that words may be given to me in opening my mouth boldly to proclaim the mystery of the gospel, for which I am an ambassador in chains, that I may declare boldly, as I ought to speak (Ephesians 6:18-20).

Continue steadfastly in prayer, being watchful in it with thanksgiving. At the same time, pray also for us, that God may open to us a door for the word, to declare the mystery of Christ, on account of which I am in prison—that I may make it clear, which is how I ought to speak (Colossians 4:2-4).

Do not be anxious about anything, but in every-thing by prayer and supplication with thanksgiving let your requests be made known to God. And the peace of God, which surpasses all understanding, will guard your hearts and your minds in Christ Jesus (Philippians 4:6-7).

Prayer forms the foundation of a continuous and growing relationship of love and devotion with the Father. Jesus speaks to this divine relationship in John 15:5: "I am the vine; you are the branches. Whoever abides in me and I in him, he it is that bears much fruit, for apart from me you can do nothing." Jesus invites every leader to experience the abundant life that comes from remaining rooted in Him. When leadership flows from this loving communion with Jesus, it becomes fruitful and life-giving. However, as Peter

Scazzero cautions, neglecting time with God leaves leaders vulnerable to burnout and spiritual defeat:

> Whenever we find ourselves wanting the ministry impact *of* Jesus while simultaneously resisting spending time *with* Jesus, we are positioning ourselves for a beating and some variation on being run "out of the house naked and bleeding."[23]

Abiding in Jesus provides the strength, encouragement, and protection necessary to navigate the pressures and challenges of ministry leadership.

Just as Jesus regularly withdrew from the demands of ministry to spend time with the Father, ministry leaders must also prioritize rest and renewal in God's presence. In this divine relationship, leaders will find the deep rest and rootedness they need to lead and serve others effectively.

LOVE: LOVE FOR OTHERS

As Jesus prepared His disciples for His departure, He issued a crucial command: "A new commandment I give to you, that you love one another: just as I have loved you, you also are to love one another. By this all people will know that you are my disciples, if you have love for one another" (John 13:34-35). This directive sets the ultimate standard for how His followers are to live and lead in His absence—by embodying love. Jesus demonstrated this love to His disciples through a powerful act of servanthood, washing their feet, and saying, "If I then, your Lord and Teacher, have washed your feet, you also ought to wash one another's feet. For I have given you an example, that you also should do just as I have done to you" (John 13:14-15).

For ministry leaders, following Jesus means loving those they lead. This love is not abstract but is expressed in tangible ways, such as being fully present with others. Henri Nouwen beautifully captures this aspect of love, saying:

> To care means first of all to be present to each other. From experience you know that those who care for you become present to you. When they listen, they listen to you. When they speak, they speak to you. Their presence is a healing presence because they accept you on your terms, and they encourage you to take your own life seriously.[24]

Leaders must recognize the inherent worth of each individual, created in the image of God, and offer them their full attention and time. Authentic connection requires intentionality, and love is demonstrated through listening deeply and speaking with kindness and respect. This kind of love is the hallmark of true discipleship and forms the foundation of effective ministry leadership.

LOVE: LOVE FOR JESUS

Paul Tripp eloquently underscores the critical role of a deep love for Jesus in the life of a ministry leader. He writes,

> The most powerful protection from the dangers that every leader faces is not his relationship to his fellow leaders but a heart that is ruled by deeply rooted love for Jesus. It is love for Jesus that has the power to crush leader pride. It is love for Jesus that ignites and protects our love for one another. It is love for Jesus that turns ministry achievement from a cause for self-glory into a reason to worship. It is love for Jesus that protects a leader from both fear of man and fear of failure.[25]

For ministry leaders, a deep love for Jesus must serve as the bedrock of their lives, shaping their behavior and driving their actions. This love goes beyond mere emotion; it is a guiding force that fundamentally influences leadership. Jesus' final conversation with Peter highlights the centrality of this love. In John 21:15-17, Jesus asks Peter three times, "Do you love me?" Each time Peter responds affirmatively, and each time Jesus gives him the command to care for His flock: "Feed my lambs," "Tend my sheep," and "Feed my sheep." Through this repetition, Jesus makes it clear that genuine love for Him must be expressed through active care for His people.

This passage reveals a profound truth: love for Jesus cannot be separated from the responsibility to lead and care for others. Jesus wanted to ensure that Peter's love for Him was genuine, and the way to prove that love was through active service to God's people. Similarly, for leaders in God's kingdom, love for Christ must be evident in their dedication to guiding, protecting, and nurturing those they lead. This devotion is not simply a duty but a reflection of their love for Jesus.

Jesus modeled this kind of love through His actions—by humbly washing His disciples' feet and ultimately laying down His life on the cross. The greatest expression of love is self-sacrifice, and as the Good Shepherd, Jesus exemplified that true leadership is about laying down one's life for others. He calls every leader to follow this example, as He did with Peter, saying, "Follow me" (John 21:19). A deep, devoted love for Jesus must compel kingdom leaders to selflessly care for His flock, embodying the sacrificial love that Jesus Himself demonstrated.

ACCOUNTABILITY

Accountability plays a crucial role in kingdom leadership, providing a vital framework for leaders to safeguard themselves from the pitfalls of sin and temptation. Paul Tripp underscores the significance of accountability, stating,

> Accountability means living as if I really do believe that isolated, individualized, independent

Christianity never produces good fruit. It means acknowledging that every leader needs to be led and every pastor needs to be pastored. It means confessing that as long as sin remains in me, and that apart from restraining grace and the rescuing ministry of those around me, I continue to be a danger to myself.[26]

Accountability involves inviting trusted individuals into the leader's life, enabling them to provide care for their soul and help maintain the safe boundaries God has established. These relationships foster transparency and allow others to identify potential areas of concern before they jeopardize the leader's integrity or credibility. By nurturing these deep, transparent relationships with fellow leaders, ministry leaders can safeguard their hearts against the unique temptations and challenges that come with their roles.

A critical aspect of accountability is proactively developing plans to address potential areas of sin, weakness, and failure. Every leader will inevitably face challenges, and preparation is essential. Billy Graham, a renowned ministry leader, understood the value of accountability deeply. To guard himself and his team from the allure of temptation, Graham crafted specific principles and boundaries known as the Modesto Manifesto. These guidelines were designed to uphold personal integrity and preserve the credibility of his ministry.

Graham recognized that credibility is indispensable to effective leadership, and he was unwavering in his commitment to protect it. Reflecting on the Modesto Manifesto, he remarked,

> In reality, it did not mark a radical departure for us; we had always held these principles. It did, however, settle in our hearts and minds, once and for all, the determination that integrity would be the hallmark of both our lives and ministry.[27]

Wise ministry leaders take deliberate steps to guard against temptation. This strategy involves establishing a network of trusted friends for transparency and accountability, along with clear guidelines that preserve the integrity of their leadership. By embedding these safeguards, leaders ensure their ministry remains grounded in integrity, allowing them to serve faithfully and lead others effectively.

KINGDOM LEADERSHIP VS. MERITOCRACY: A CALL TO CHRIST-CENTERED MINISTRY

Leadership in the kingdom of God is distinct from secular leadership because it is divinely authorized, directed, and empowered by God Himself. Kingdom leaders are His ambassadors, entrusted with spiritual authority and influence to fulfill His purposes. This divine commissioning sets kingdom leadership apart, giving it a sacred weight that transcends any earthly leadership model. Faithful ministry leaders bring honor to God when they steward this responsibility with wisdom, leading His people and advancing His mission. Scholars Benjamin Forrest and David Nemitz rightly state,

> Being called by God to be his ambassador, to lead his people or to lead other people to him is a high and holy calling. Because of this honor, invest intently in the tasks before you and work to understand the demands that Scripture places on you.[28]

In this context, kingdom leadership is not simply about leading others; it's about embodying gospel-centered values and carrying out God's will with integrity, humility, and unwavering devotion.

New Testament scholar and theologian Scot McKnight and author Laura Barringer offer a powerful critique of the modern evangelical church, noting that over the past fifty years, a radical shift has occurred. They argue that, "The American meritocracy has reshaped pastors and churches, and a new culture has taken root, based on achievement and accomplishment rather than holiness and Christlikeness."[29] In this meritocratic system, moral values are often redefined in economic terms. Character is no longer measured by love, service, and care but by traits such as grit, productivity, and self-discipline. This approach transforms the church into a competitive environment, where individuals strive for recognition rather than spiritual growth.

McKnight and Barringer further describe the impact of this shift on the church:

> Churches today have been so greatly influenced by meritocracy, by the achievement and accomplishment culture of the business world, that they now define *pastor* with business-culture terms instead of biblical terms. In business terms, a pastor is a "leader," and *leader* is defined by the meritocratic system of American culture. But when pastors are defined primarily as *leaders*—or *entrepreneurs* or *visionaries*—they've already ceased to be pastors in any biblical sense. Further, when the church becomes an *institution* or *organization*—or worse, a *corporation*—it ceases to be a church (that is, a vital part of the body of Christ). Moreover, "pastor as leader" blurs the lines of headship in the church, and people begin to lose sight of the church's one true and only head, Jesus Christ.[30]

This merit-based culture often pressures pastors to focus on performance metrics and measurable achievements, which diverges from the example Jesus set. Scripture consistently portrays Christ as the ultimate model for leadership—one centered on humility, service, and transformation, not performance. The primary goal of pastors and ministry leaders should be to reflect Christlikeness. As ambassadors of Christ, they are called to lead others toward this same transformation. Every pastor and ministry leader should aspire to embody *Christoformity* —the reflection of Christ's character—and lead others along this spiritual path. Jesus' life and ministry provide the perfect blueprint for nurturing God's people toward genuine spiritual formation.

CHRIST-CENTERED LEADERSHIP: EMBRACING THE MODEL OF THE GOOD SHEPHERD

Serving as a pastor or ministry leader in the American church is a challenging calling. American cultural values permeate every aspect of society, including the church, and pastors and ministry leaders are not immune to these secular pressures. The weight of expectations and the drive for measurable success can cause many church leaders to lose sight of their biblically defined role, leading some to adopt secular models that prioritize achievement and metrics, transforming churches into business-like entities. McKnight and Barringer caution against this approach, warning,

> It turns pastors into leaders whose primary aim is the success of the organization based in some way on achievable metrics. The more ambitious the leader and the more narcissistic the leader, the less of a church the church becomes.[31]

In contrast, churches need pastors and leaders who serve under the guidance of the Good Shepherd, growing in their own Christlikeness and guiding the congregation to do the same. The true goal is to become more like Jesus, with a focus on redemption and restoration rather than profit, position, or power. In God's kingdom, Christlikeness—not worldly success—is the ultimate measure of achievement.

Pastoral leadership stands apart from other forms of leadership because ministry leaders are, first and foremost, followers of Jesus. They are called to fulfill their responsibilities within a society that often promotes values and principles that frequently conflict with—and even oppose—the kingdom of God. Pastor and theologian Eugene Peterson captures this tension well, writing:

> I don't love rampant consumerism that treats God as a product to be marketed. I don't love the dehumanizing ways that turn men, women, and children into impersonal roles and causes and statistics. I don't love the competitive spirit that treats others as rivals and even as enemies. The cultural conditions in which I am immersed require, at least for me, a kind of fierce vigilance to guard my vocation from these cultural pollutants so dangerously toxic to persons who want to follow Jesus in the way that he is Jesus. I wanted my life, both my

personal and working life, to be shaped by God and the scriptures and prayer.[32]

The ultimate example of leadership is found in the Lord Himself, who provides a perfect model for leading others. Psalm 23 vividly portrays the Lord as a shepherd-leader, setting the standard for how shepherds are to care for His people. He is the chief mentor and guide, demonstrating how to shepherd the flock with sacrificial love and care. The Lord is the Great Shepherd of all undershepherds, and any authority or influence they hold comes from Him alone.

What sets Christian leadership apart is that all authority originates with God, the King, who entrusts His undershepherds with a portion of His authority to serve His people. Shepherd-leaders submit their will to the Lord, fulfilling their role in service to Him and under His guidance. Forrest and Nemitz capture this concept well:

> True Christian leadership never sets a new course; it is always directionally oriented because it is following the charge of the King. Christian leadership and leaders receive their commissioning from the King, and use their authority *for* accomplishing his purposes. Therefore, in God's position as King, he has granted leaders the opportunity to serve. We, as leaders and subjects of this King, serve on his behalf. We are stewards of what he has tasked us with

and in this way we are always directionally focused, keeping a watch on our bearing and trajectories, making sure that our leadership is in accordance with our manifest.[33]

The example of Christ demonstrates that this service to the Lord must be carried out with humility and selflessness, reflecting the heart of a servant-shepherd (Philippians 2:1-11). Christ's model calls kingdom leaders to a life of service that honors God and nurtures His people, prioritizing spiritual transformation over personal ambition.

THE TRUE VINE

I am the true vine, and my Father is the vinedresser. Every branch in me that does not bear fruit he takes away, and every branch that does bear fruit he prunes, that it may bear more fruit. Already you are clean because of the word that I have spoken to you. Abide in me, and I in you. As the branch cannot bear fruit by itself, unless it abides in the vine, neither can you, unless you abide in me. I am the vine; you are the branches. Whoever abides in me and I in him, he it is that bears much fruit, for apart from me you can do nothing. If anyone does not abide in me he is thrown away like a branch and withers; and the branches are gathered, thrown into the fire, and burned. If you abide in me, and my words abide in you, ask whatever you wish, and it will be done for you.

- John 15:1-7

Chapter Nine

ABIDING IN CHRIST

The Essential Foundation for
Kingdom Leadership

As the time of His crucifixion approached, Jesus shifted His focus to a crucial task: preparing His disciples for the moment when He would no longer be physically present with them. The weight of this moment is unmistakable in the chapters leading up to John 15, where Jesus, fully aware of His impending betrayal and death, speaks to His disciples with a sense of profound urgency. In John 13:33, He says, "Yet a little while I am with you. You will seek me, and just as I said to the Jews, so now I also say to you, 'Where I am going you cannot come.'" Jesus knew that their world was about to be turned upside down, and the future that they had envisioned was about to unravel. The Teacher they had faithfully followed and pinned their hopes on would soon be gone. This looming reality left the disciples overwhelmed with confusion, devastation, and intense anxiety.

In His compassion and foresight, Jesus understood the trials and challenges His disciples would soon face in His absence. To prepare them for the mission ahead, He took two pivotal steps. First, He provided comfort and reassurance, soothing their fears and fortifying their faith. Second, He imparted a critical teaching that would sustain them in the difficult days to come: the necessity of abiding in Him.

The teaching in John 15:1-7 is far more than a suggestion or gentle encouragement; it is a declaration of paramount importance. Jesus didn't simply speak these words—He issued a command, one that their survival, faithfulness, and fruitfulness in carrying out His mission would hinge upon. He proclaimed,

> I am the true vine, and my Father is the vinedresser. Every branch in me that does not bear fruit he takes away, and every branch that does bear fruit he prunes, that it may bear more fruit. Already you are clean because of the word that I have spoken to you. Abide in me, and I in you. As the branch cannot bear fruit by itself, unless it abides in the vine, neither can you, unless you abide in me. I am the vine; you are the branches. Whoever abides in me and I in him, he it is that bears much fruit, for apart from me you can do nothing. If anyone does not abide in me he is thrown away like a branch and withers; and the branches are gathered, thrown into the fire, and burned. If you abide in me, and my words abide in you, ask whatever you wish, and it will be done for you.

This message is not limited to the disciples of Jesus' time but echoes through the ages, speaking directly to leaders today. God calls kingdom leaders to carry forward the mission of Christ, yet like the disciples, they cannot fulfill this calling through their own strength or wisdom. The teaching of abiding in Christ remains as vital as ever, serving as the foundation for effective, faithful, and fruitful leadership.

This chapter explores the profound significance of abiding in Jesus—what it truly means, why it's crucial, and how it influences every dimension of a leader's life and mission. Abiding in Christ is not just a theological idea; it is the very lifeblood of kingdom leadership and the key to fulfilling the mission God has entrusted to His leaders. As this essential foundation is examined, it becomes clear that the call to abide in Jesus is both an invitation and a command, carrying the promise of a life that reflects Christ's character and brings glory to the Father.

THE SIGNIFICANCE OF ABIDING

To abide means to endure, to continue, to remain steadfast. Using the image of the vine and branches, Jesus vividly illustrates the vital connection leaders must maintain with Him. Abiding in Jesus extends far beyond a superficial relationship; it requires cultivating an intimate, life-giving connection that sustains and transforms.

Abiding in Jesus is the only way leaders can produce genuine, lasting fruit. This relationship requires ongoing, wholehearted dependence on Christ's indwelling presence. When a leader abides in Him, Jesus becomes the inner source that empowers, directs, and teaches, shaping their life and leadership.

The Apostle Paul captured the essence of this indwelling relationship in Galatians 2:20, when he proclaimed, "I have been crucified with Christ. It is no longer I who live, but Christ who lives in me." Paul's actions were driven by Christ living through him, not by his own desires or authority.

Leadership in God's kingdom is authorized, empowered, guided, and sustained by abiding in Jesus. It requires surrendering to His authority and allowing Him to lead. The danger with self-leadership lies in the temptation to believe one can lead effectively through personal strength and interests. In the world's view, self-leadership means turning authority inward, relying solely on oneself. But kingdom leaders are called to a higher standard. Their leadership must not be rooted in self-reliance, but in a life-giving connection with Jesus, the True Vine. The only valid form of self-leadership for kingdom leaders is the deliberate effort to lead themselves into deeper dependence on Christ, trusting Him as their sole source of strength and direction.

THE MODEL OF ABIDING: JESUS AND THE FATHER

Jesus exemplifies the perfect example of an abiding relationship through His deep and unwavering connection with the Father. He invites His followers to observe and imitate this relationship. In John 14:10, Jesus declares, "Do you not believe that I am in the Father and the Father is in me? The words that I say to you I do not speak on my own authority, but the Father who dwells in me does his works." His life was characterized by absolute dependence on the Father; He did nothing apart from Him. This profound connection is reflected in the following passages:

John 8:28 – When you have lifted up the Son of Man, then you will know that I am he, and that I do nothing on my own authority, but speak just as the Father taught me.

John 5:19 – Truly, truly, I say to you, the Son can do nothing of his own accord, but only what he sees the Father doing. For whatever the Father does, that the Son does likewise.

These verses highlight the depth of Jesus' reliance on the Father, establishing the standard for how leaders should align their lives. Daily prayer and practice should reflect this attitude: "I can do nothing on my own, but only what I see the Father doing. For whatever the Father does, that I do likewise."

To discern the Father's will, one must immerse themselves in scripture, carefully studying the life of Jesus and observing how He responded and acted in various situations.

Leaders are also called to seek God's wisdom, guidance, and revelation through prayer: "Lord, show me what you want me to do and tell me what you want me to say."

If Jesus Himself did nothing apart from the Father, leaders must also live in a state of continuous dependence on Him. Jesus demonstrates that true authority flows from the Father, and kingdom leaders are called to follow His example by aligning their actions and words with the Father's will. This kind of obedience and alignment can only be achieved through an intimate, abiding relationship with Jesus.

PERSEVERANCE IN ABIDING

Abiding in Jesus involves becoming a dwelling place for the Father, Son, and Holy Spirit. This relationship requires perseverance, as one must remain in Him despite counterinfluences, opposition, or discouragement. It demands making Jesus the priority, understanding that challenges will arise to pull leaders away from Him. Kingdom leaders, in particular, will face trials in this area but must remain steadfast, committed to staying rooted in Christ no matter what comes their way.

Abiding in Jesus nurtures a deep, personal relationship, allowing a leader to know Him intimately. As one grows closer to Him, they become more familiar with His character, and this closeness shapes them, leading them to reflect the "fruit" of His character in their own lives. Leaders will always produce the fruit of what they choose to abide in.

By remaining in Jesus, they naturally bear His fruit. Abiding goes beyond simply following Him; it means walking with Him and living in close communion with Him. To walk with Jesus, one must first truly know Him, and this knowledge is gained through abiding. The result of this intimate relationship is a life that bears fruit, visibly identifying one as His disciple, which ultimately brings glory to the Father.

THE CHOICE TO ABIDE

Leaders have many options for where they place their trust, but only by abiding in Jesus can they produce the fruit of His character. As representatives of the King, He must be their life source. Jesus is the only true and lasting answer to their deepest needs. Abiding in Him is a deliberate choice, one that demands a clear decision because it is of utmost importance—it is either a commitment to remain in Jesus, or to seek fulfillment elsewhere. There is no middle ground.

When leaders choose to abide in Jesus, they embrace a path of complete and continual dependence on Him. Though it may be costly, it bears the fruit of Christ's character. Conversely, choosing not to abide in Jesus leads to reliance on self or other things, which results in disobedience, spiritual barrenness, and ultimately, judgment and death—robbing God of the glory that rightfully belongs to Him.

UNDERSTANDING FRUIT

Vine's *Expository Dictionary of New Testament Words* defines fruit as "the visible expression of power working inwardly and invisibly, and the character of the fruit is the evidence of the character of the power producing it."[1] For leaders who abide in Jesus, it is His power at work within them, and the fruit they bear will be a reflection of His character.

This fruit encompasses every aspect of a leader's life and ministry; it is impossible to separate personal conduct from ministry work. Leaders must ensure that both their private lives and public ministries consistently reflect the character of God and bring glory to Him in all things.

To grow in fruitfulness, leaders must actively listen to and respond to Jesus' teachings; this process involves being pruned, cleansed, and purified. Bearing fruit as Christ's followers requires ongoing dependence on Jesus, communion with Him through the Holy Spirit, and submission to His will in all things. Abiding in Jesus leads to the production of genuine, abundant fruit that mirrors His character.

THE CONSEQUENCES OF FRUITLESSNESS

Fruitless plants are ultimately useless, as Jesus vividly illustrates in Luke 13:6-7 through the parable of the barren fig tree. In the story, a man seeks fruit from a fig tree he planted in his vineyard, but after three years of finding none, he orders it to be cut down, asking, "Why should it use up the ground?" The tree, without fruit, serves no purpose, occupying space without fulfilling its intended function.

For leaders, this parable is a stark and sobering reminder. Scripture makes it clear that leaders are ineffective and useless if they are not bearing the fruit of Christ. Their spiritual vitality is entirely dependent on their connection to Jesus. Without this lifeline, they face spiritual decay. Jesus amplifies this warning in John 15:6, where He states, "If anyone does not abide in me he is thrown away like a branch and withers; and the branches are gathered, thrown into the fire, and burned."

A leader's best effort, apart from God's enablement, is worthless. Without the life source of The Vine, they will quickly die, and dead branches are worthless for building. How can they build the kingdom of God if they are dead and worthless?

THE GIFT OF THE HOLY SPIRIT

When Jesus prepared to leave His disciples, He made a profound promise: to send them a Helper, the Holy Spirit. In John 14:16-17, 26, Jesus reassures them by saying,

> And I will ask the Father, and he will give you another Helper, to be with you forever, even the Spirit of truth, whom the world cannot receive, because it neither sees him nor knows him. You know him, for he dwells with you and will be in you. But the

Helper, the Holy Spirit, whom the Father will send in my name, he will teach you all things and bring to your remembrance all that I have said to you.

The gift of the Holy Spirit is not merely a temporary provision, but a permanent indwelling presence meant to guide and empower leaders in their obedience to Christ and fulfillment of His mission. Through the Holy Spirit, Jesus remains with His followers, offering divine support, wisdom, and strength. This constant presence ensures that leaders are never alone in their calling, but are equipped with the supernatural help necessary to walk in alignment with Christ's purpose and to lead others faithfully.

KINGDOM LEADERSHIP AND SELF-LEADERSHIP

Self-leadership in God's kingdom is not about being self-absorbed, self-sufficient, or self-empowered. Leaders who focus on themselves and operate independently of God end up placing themselves at the center of their own universe, relegating Jesus to the sidelines.

In ministry leadership, there is an ongoing struggle between the kingdom of self and the kingdom of God. When individuals place their personal desires and ambitions at the forefront, they are effectively building their own kingdom. Yet, in the true kingdom of God, there is only one King—Jesus. He made it clear in Matthew 6:24, "No one can serve two masters, for either he will hate the one and love the other, or he will be devoted to the one and despise the other."

It is impossible to be self-absorbed and simultaneously call Jesus King. As Jeremy Treat wisely observes in *Seek First: How the Kingdom of God Changes Everything*, "Here's the truth: when we don't give everything over to Jesus, we're still the one who is in control. We act as our own king and then try to use Jesus to accomplish our goals."[2]

Self-leadership, when focused on personal desires, emotions, ambitions, and recognition, revolves entirely around the individual. Kingdom leadership, however, is rooted in abiding in Jesus and seeking God's glory above all else. True identity, security, hope, well-being, meaning, and purpose come from complete dependence on Him alone, not from self-reliance.

THE IMPORTANCE OF INTIMACY WITH GOD

Leaders must acknowledge their desperate need for God's wisdom and power to guide them, for without Him, they can accomplish nothing. Intimacy with God is the bedrock of effective leadership. Leaders should actively seek and experience His presence through the spiritual disciplines of prayer, solitude, worship, and engaging deeply with scripture. These practices help leaders surrender control, enabling God to direct their lives and decisions. Abiding in Him becomes the source of strength and resilience, equipping them to meet the demands of leadership.

Rather than being overwhelmed by challenges, leaders should let difficulties drive them toward greater dependence on God—recognizing Him as their lifeline and source of sustained strength. Jesus modeled this principle beautifully by prioritizing time in God's presence, knowing that His life and ministry depended entirely on His connection with the Father. His life was filled with moments of solitude and prayer, where He experienced transformative encounters with God that refreshed and fortified His soul.

Jesus extends the same invitation to every leader, calling them to experience the abundant life that flows from Him. When leadership is born out of this loving communion with Jesus, it becomes both fruitful and life-giving. Abiding in Christ creates space for God to renew and fill leaders, providing strength, encouragement, and protection needed to navigate the pressures and challenges of leadership with grace and purpose.

THE INVITATION TO ABIDE

Kingdom leadership revolves around one foundational principle: abiding in Christ. Just as Jesus emphasized to His disciples before His departure, the very lifeblood of effective ministry is found in remaining deeply connected to Him. Without this relationship, leaders risk becoming spiritually barren, ineffective, and cut off from their true source of strength. Jesus' teaching in John 15 is not a mere suggestion but a command, as vital for leaders today as it was for His original followers. Through abiding in Christ, leaders are empowered, refined, and made fruitful, reflecting His character and faithfully fulfilling the mission entrusted to them.

The model for this abiding relationship is found in Jesus' own dependence on the Father. In following His example, kingdom leaders are called to a life of complete reliance on God, not on themselves. This reliance produces fruit—not only in personal character but also in ministry effectiveness. However, it requires perseverance, intentionality, and a steadfast commitment to prioritize an intimate relationship with Jesus.

God provides everything leaders need to be fruitful, both in their personal lives and in their leadership roles, if they choose to abide in Him. He has entrusted them with unique gifts and anointing to lead for His glory, and it is their responsibility to steward these gifts in a way that honors Him. The only way to achieve this goal is by walking closely with Him and depending on Him as their ultimate source of strength and direction.

The Holy Spirit has been given to guide, teach, and empower leaders in their abiding relationship with Christ, offering the necessary strength to face the challenges of ministry. Leaders must daily recognize their need for God's wisdom, power, and presence, and allow this dependence to shape both their lives and their leadership.

Ultimately, the call to abide in Christ is both an invitation and a command—a promise of a life and leadership that glorifies God. Leaders who choose to remain in Him will not only find the strength to lead but also experience the joy and fulfillment that comes from bearing fruit for the kingdom. God's invitation is clear: come and abide. He will provide everything needed to thrive in both life and leadership, but only through an ongoing, intimate connection with Christ.

NOTES

Chapter 1
THE CHURCH'S LEADERSHIP DILEMMA
Navigating Secularization and Reclaiming Biblical Principles

1. J.B. Watson Jr. and Walter H Scalen Jr., "'Dining with the Devil': The Unique Secularization of American Evangelical Churches," *International Social Science Review* 83, no. 3/4 (2008): 174.

2. Alan Wolfe, *The Transformation of American Religion: How We Actually Live Our Faith* (New York: Free Press, 2003), 3.

3. Tracy Munsil, "US Christians Embrace Secularism in 'Post-Christian' America," Arizona Christian University, October 6, 2020, http://www.arizonachristian.edu/2020/10/06/us-christians-embrace-secularism-in-post-christian-america/.

4. George Barna, "American Worldview Inventory 2020 Results—FULL Release #11: Churches and Worldview," Cultural Research Center, Arizona Christian University, October 6, 2020, https://www.arizonachristian.edu/wp.content/uploads/2020/10/CRC_AWVI2020_Release11_Digital_04_20201006. pdf.

5. Munsil, "US Christians Embrace Secularism."

6. Watson and Scalen, "'Dining with the Devil,'" 171-180.

7. Reggie McNeal, *The Present Future: Six Tough Questions for the Church* (San Francisco, CA: Jossey-Bass, 2003), 22-23.

8. McNeal, *The Present Future*, 23-25.

9. Leah MarieAnn Klett, "Crisis in Church Leadership: How Celebrity Pastors Can Avoid Failing the Fame Test," *The Christian Post*, October 10, 2021, https://www.christianpost.com/news/how-christian-celebrities-can-avoid-failing-the-fame-test.html.

10. Michael Gryboski, "'Pandemic of Narcissism': Seminaries Respond to the Evangelical Church Leadership Crisis," *The Christian Post*, October 9, 2021, https://www.christianpost.com/news/seminaries-respond-to-the-evangelical-church-leadership-crisis.html.

11. Richard L Mayhue, "Authentic Spiritual Leadership," *The Master's Seminary Journal* 22, no. 2 (2011): 213-224.

12. Joseph M. Stowell, *Redefining Leadership: Character-Driven Habits of Effective Leaders* (Grand Rapids, MI: Zondervan, 2017), 50.

13. Paul David Tripp, *Lead: 12 Gospel Principles for Leadership in the Church* (Wheaton, Illinois: Crossway, 2020), 109.

Chapter 2
LEADERSHIP AND POWER
Navigating Influence with Biblical Integrity

1. Benjamin Forrest and Chet Roden, eds., *Biblical Leadership: Theology for the Everyday Leader* (Grand Rapids, MI: Kregel Academic, 2017), 9.

2. Peter G. Northouse, *Leadership: Theory and Practice*, 8th ed. (Thousand Oaks, CA: SAGE Publications, Inc., 2019), 9.

3. James MacGregor Burns, *Leadership* (New York, NY: Harper & Row, 1978).

4. Robert A. Dahl, "The Concept of Power," *Behavioral Science* 2, no. 3 (1957): 201-215.

5. W. Graham Astley and Paramjit S. Sachdeva, "Structural Sources of Intraorganizational Power: A Theoretical Synthesis," *Academy of Management Review* 9, no. 1 (January 1984): 104-113; Abraham Kaplan, "Power in Perspective," in *Power and Conflict in Organizations*, eds. Robert L. Kahn and Elise Boulding (London, England: Tavistock, 1964), 11-32.

6. Joanne B. Ciulla, "Ethics and Effectiveness: The Nature of Good Leadership," in *The Nature of Leadership*, eds. John Antonakis and David V. Day, 3rd ed. (Thousand Oaks, CA: SAGE Publications, Inc., 2017), 460.

7. Sturm and Monzani, "Power and Leadership," 292.

Chapter 3
THE KINGDOM OF GOD
A Central Biblical Theme

1. J. D. Douglas and Merrill C. Tenney, *Zondervan Illustrated Bible Dictionary*, ed. Moisés Silva, Illustrated ed. (Grand Rapids, MI: Zondervan Academic, 2011), 811.

2. George Eldon Ladd, *Gospel of the Kingdom: Scriptural Studies in the Kingdom of God* (Grand Rapids, MI: Eerdmans Publishing Co., 1990), 19.

3. Douglas and Tenney, *Zondervan Illustrated Bible Dictionary*, 809.

4. Ladd, *Gospel of the Kingdom*, 20.

5. Martyn Lloyd-Jones, *The Kingdom of God* (Wheaton, IL: Crossway, 2010), 98-99.

6. Lloyd-Jones, *The Kingdom of God*, 200.

Chapter 4
JESUS AND THE KINGDOM OF GOD

1. Origen, *The Complete Works of Origen*, trans. Philip Schaff (Omaha, NE: Patristic Publishing, 2017), 1556-1557.

2. Jürgen Moltmann, "Jesus And The Kingdom of God," *The Asbury Journal* 48, no. 1 (January 1, 1993), https://place.asburyseminary.edu/asburyjournal/vol48/iss1/2, 5.

3. D. A. Carson, Walter W. Wessel, and Walter L. Liefeld, *The Expositor's Bible Commentary: Matthew, Mark, Luke, with the New International Version of the Holy Bible*, ed. Frank E. Gaebelein (London: Zondervan, 1984), 181-82.

4. F. B. Meyer, *Inherit the Kingdom: Meditations on the Sermon on the Mount* (Wheaton, IL: Victor Books, 1985), 30.

Chapter 5
CHARACTERISTICS OF THE KINGDOM OF GOD

1. Athanasius, *Life of St Antony*, trans. Robert T. Meyer (London, England: Longmans, Green & Co., 1950), 37.

2. Alister E. McGrath, *Christian Theology: An Introduction*, 6th ed. (Chichester, West Sussex: John Wiley & Sons Ltd., 2017), 272.

3. C. S. Lewis, *Mere Christianity* (San Francisco: HarperOne, 2015), 116.

4. Wayne Grudem, *Systematic Theology: An Introduction to Biblical Doctrine*, 2nd ed. (Grand Rapids, MI: Zondervan Academic, 2020), 1523.

5. Merrill C. Tenney and Moisés Silva, *The Zondervan Encyclopedia of the Bible*, vol. 5, *Q-Z* (Zondervan, 2009), 129.

6. Mathetes, *Epistle to Diognetus*, trans. Alexander Roberts and James Donaldson (Buffalo, NY: The Christian Literature Company, 1885), 15.

7. Tenney and Silva, *The Zondervan Encyclopedia of the Bible*, 144.

8. Ladd, *Gospel of the Kingdom*, 47.

9. Origen, *Origen on Prayer*, ed. William Curtis (Chicago, IL: Letcetera Publishing, 2015), 11.

10. Benedicta Ward, ed., *The Desert Fathers: Sayings of the Early Christian Monks*, Rev. ed. (London, England: Penguin Classics, 2003), 231.

Chapter 6

KINGDOM LEADERSHIP
Urgency, Transformation, and the Cost of Discipleship

1. Craig S. Keener, *The IVP Bible Background Commentary: New Testament* (Westmont, IL: InterVarsity Press, 1994), 173.

2. John R. W. Stott, *Christian Counter-Culture: The Message of the Sermon on the Mount* (Downers Grove, IL: InterVarsity Press, 1978), 18.

3. Robert Wayne Stacy, "Following Jesus in the Kingdom of God: Leadership in the Synoptic Gospels," in *Biblical Leadership*, eds. Benjamin Forrest and Chet Roden (Grand Rapids, MI: Kregel Academic, 2017), 319.

4. Stacy, "Following Jesus in the Kingdom," 321.

5. Douglas Petersen, "Kingdom Rules: Upside-down Discipleship," *Asian Journal of Pentecostal Studies* 16, no. 1 (January 2013): 31-50.

6. Stacy, "Following Jesus in the Kingdom, " 325.

7. R. Alan Cole, *Mark* (Downers Grove, IL: IVP Academic, 2008), 247.

8. C. Gene Wilkes and Calvin Miller, *Jesus on Leadership: Timeless Wisdom on Servant Leadership* (Wheaton, IL: Tyndale House Publishers, Inc., 1998), 175.

9. Petersen, "Kingdom Rules," 38-39.

10. Jeremy R. Treat, *Seek First: How the Kingdom of God Changes Everything* (Grand Rapids, MI: Zondervan, 2019), 65.

11. Treat, *Seek First*, 23, 25.

Chapter 7

A BIBLICAL MODEL OF LEADERSHIP
Shepherd Leadership

1. Craig S. Keener and John H. Walton, eds., *NIV Cultural Backgrounds Study Bible: Bringing to Life the Ancient World of Scripture*, special ed. (Grand Rapids, MI: Zondervan, 2016), 1388.

2. Frank Damazio, *The Making of a Leader* (Portland, OR: City Bible Publishing, 1988), 89-90.

3. W. Phillip Keller, *A Shepherd Looks at Psalm 23* (Grand Rapids, MI: Zondervan, 1970), 121.

4. Timothy S. Laniak, *Shepherds After My Own Heart: Pastoral Traditions and Leadership in the Bible* (Downers Grove, IL: InterVarsity Press, 2006), 248.

5. St. Augustine, *Sermo 46*, 1-2: CCL 41, 529-30.

6. Damazio, *The Making of a Leader*, 91.

7. Laniak, *Shepherds After My Own Heart*, 114.

8. Walter C. Kaiser Jr., "The 'Shepherd' as a Biblical Metaphor: Leadership in Psalm 23," in *Biblical Leadership: Theology for the Everyday Leader*, eds. Benjamin Forrest and Chet Roden (Grand Rapids, MI: Kregel Academic, 2017), 161.

9. Damazio, *The Making of a Leader*, 75.

10. Keller, *A Shepherd Looks at Psalm 23*, 19.

11. Paul David Tripp, *Dangerous Calling: Confronting the Unique Challenges of Pastoral Ministry*, 1st ed. (Wheaton, IL: Crossway, 2012), 98.

Chapter 8

FOUNDATIONAL CHARACTERISTICS OF KINGDOM LEADERSHIP

1. Stacy, "Following Jesus in the Kingdom of God," 319-320.

2. Tripp, *Lead*, 22-23.

3. Tripp, *Lead*, 22.

4. D. A. Carson, *The Gospel According to John*, reprint ed. (Grand Rapids, MI: Eerdmans Publishing Co., 1990), 251.

5. Harold Myra and Marshall Shelley, *The Leadership Secrets of Billy Graham* (Grand Rapids, MI: Zondervan, 2008), 19.

6. Myra and Shelley, *The Leadership Secrets of Billy Graham*, 31.

7. Tripp, *Lead*, 135.

8. Stacy, *"Following Jesus in the Kingdom of God,"* 324.

9. George Barna, ed., *Leaders on Leadership: Wisdom, Advice and Encouagement on the Art of Leading God's People* (Ventura, CA: Regal, 1998), 111.

10. Peter Scazzero, *Emotionally Healthy Discipleship: Moving from Shallow Christianity to Deep Transformation* (Grand Rapids, MI: Zondervan, 2021), 72.

11. Walter C. Wright, *Relational Leadership: A Biblical Model for Leadership Service*, corr. 3rd printing ed. (Carlisle, England: Paternoster, 2000), 83.

12. Tripp, *Lead*, 115-116.

13. Tripp, *Lead*, 115.

14. John Stott, *The Message of Galatians* (Westmont, IL: IVP Academic, 1968), 265.

15. Tripp, *Lead*, 123.

16. John F. Carter, "Power and Authority in Pentecostal Leadership," *Asian Journal of Pentecostal Studies* 12, no. 2 (July 2009): 186.

17. James B. Shelton, *Mighty in Word & Deed: The Role of the Holy Spirit in Luke-Acts* (Eugene, OR: Wipf and Stock, 2000), 65.

18. Myra and Shelley, *The Leadership Secrets of Billy Graham*, 51.

19. Scazzero, *Emotionally Healthy Discipleship*, 54.

20. Ruth Haley Barton, *Strengthening the Soul of Your Leadership: Seeking God in the Crucible of Ministry* (Downers Grove, IL: InterVarsity Press, 2008), 16.

21. Henri J. M. Nouwen, *The Way of the Heart: Desert Spirituality and Contemporary Ministry* (New York, NY: HarperCollins, 1981), 30.

22. Richard J. Foster, *Celebration of Discipline: The Path to Spiritual Growth Special 20th Anniversary Edition* (San Francisco, CA: Harper San Francisco, 2000), 33.

23. Peter Scazzero, *The Emotionally Healthy Leader: How Transforming Your Inner Life Will Deeply Transform Your Church, Team, and the World*, illustrated ed. (Grand Rapids, MI: Zondervan, 2015), 130.

24. Henri J. M. Nouwen, *Out of Solitude: Three Meditations on the Christian Life*, rev. ed. (Notre Dame, IN: Ave Maria Press, 2004), 36.

25. Tripp, *Lead*, 56.

26. Tripp, *Lead*, 25.

27. Myra and Shelley, *The Leadership Secrets of Billy Graham*, 57.

28. Benjamin K. Forrest and David Nemitz, "Toward a Biblical Theology of Leadership: Shepherds and Servants on Behalf of the King," in *Biblical Leadership*, eds. Benjamin Forrest and Chet Roden (Grand Rapids, MI: Kregel Academic, 2017), 517.

29. Scot McKnight and Laura Barringer, *A Church Called Tov: Forming a Goodness Culture That Resists Abuses of Power and Promotes Healing* (Carol Stream, IL: Tyndale Elevate, 2020), 201.

30. McKnight and Barringer, *A Church Called Tov*, 203.

31. McKnight and Barringer, *A Church Called Tov*, 204-205.

32. Eugene H. Peterson, *The Pastor: A Memoir*, reprint ed. (San Francisco, CA: HarperOne, 2012), 5.

33. Forrest and Nemitz, "Toward a Biblical Theology of Leadership," 515.

Chapter 9
ABIDING IN CHRIST
The Essential Foundation for Kingdom Leadership

1. W.E. Vine, *Vine's Expository Dictionary of New Testament Words* (2012), 15147, Kindle.

2. Treat, *Seek First*, 65.

BIBLIOGRAPHY

Antonakis, John, and David V. Day. "Leadership: Past, Present, and Future." In *The Nature of Leadership*, edited by John Antonakis and David V. Day. Thousand Oaks, CA: SAGE Publications, Inc., 2017.

———, eds. *The Nature of Leadership*. 3rd ed. Thousand Oaks, CA: SAGE Publications, Inc., 2018.

Astley, W. Graham, and Paramjit S. Sachdeva. "Structural Sources of Intraorganizational: Power: A Theoretical Synthesis." *Academy of Management Review* 9, no. 1 (January 1984): 104-113.

Athanasius. *Life of St Antony*. Translated by Robert T. Meyer. London, England: Longmans, Green & Co., 1950.

Barna, George. "American Worldview Inventory 2020 Results—FULL Release #11: Churches and Worldview." *Cultural Research Center Arizona Christian University*. October 6, 2020. https://www.arizonachristian.edu/wp-content/uploads/2020/10/CRC_AWVI2020_Release11_Digital_04_20201006.pdf.

———, ed. *Leaders on Leadership: Wisdom, Advice and Encouragement on the Art of Leading God's People*. Ventura, CA: Regal, 1998.

Barton, Ruth Haley. *Strengthening the Soul of Your Leadership: Seeking God in the Crucible of Ministry*. Downers Grove, IL: InterVarsity Press, 2008.

Bendahan, Samuel, Christian Zehnder, François P. Pralong, and John Antonakis. "Leader Corruption Depends on Power and Testosterone." *The Leadership Quarterly* 26 (2015): 101-122.

Blackaby, Henry T., and Richard Blackaby. *Spiritual Leadership: Moving People on to God's Agenda*. Rev. ed. Nashville, TN: B&H Books, 2011.

Block, Daniel I. *The Book of Ezekiel, Chapters 25-48*. Grand Rapids, MI: Eerdmans Publishing Co., 1998.

Brooks, David. *The Second Mountain: The Quest for a Moral Life*. New York, NY: Random House Trade Paperbacks, 2020.

Bruce, F. F. *The Epistle to the Galatians*. The New International Greek Testament Commentary. Reprint ed., Eerdmans Publishing Co., 2013.

———. *The Gospel of John: Introduction, Exposition, and Notes*. Grand Rapids, MI: Eerdmans Publishing Co., 2018.

Burns, James MacGregor. *Leadership*. New York, NY: Harper & Row, 1978.

Carson, D. A. *The Gospel According to John*. Reprint ed., Grand Rapids, MI: Eerdmans Publishing Co., 1990.

Carson, D. A., Walter W. Wessel, and Walter L. Liefeld. *The Expositor's Bible Commentary : Matthew, Mark, Luke, with the New International Version of the Holy Bible*. Edited by Frank E. Gaebelein. Grand Rapids, MI: Zondervan, 1984.

Carter, John F. "Power and Authority in Pentecostal Leadership." *Asian Journal of Pentecostal Studies* 12, no. 2 (July 2009): 185-207.

Cialdini, Robert B. "Harnessing the Science of Persuasion." *Harvard Business Review*, October 1, 2001.

Cialdini, Robert B., and Noah J. Goldstein. "Social Influence: Compliance and Conformity." *Annual Review of Psychology* 55 (2004): 591-621.

Ciulla, Joanne B. "Ethics and Effectiveness: The Nature of Good Leadership." In *The Nature of Leadership*, edited by John Antonakis and David V. Day. 3rd ed. Thousand Oaks, CA: SAGE Publications, Inc., 2017.

Cole, R. Alan. *Mark*. Tyndale New Testament Commentaries. Downers Grove, IL: IVP Academic, 2008.

Collins, Jim. *Good to Great: Why Some Companies Make the Leap and Others Don't*. 1st ed. New York, NY: HarperCollins Publishers Inc., 2001.

Copeland, Norman. *Psychology and the Soldier: The Art of Leadership*. 1st ed. The Military Service Publishing Company, 1942.

Covey, Stephen M. R. *Trust and Inspire: How Truly Great Leaders Unleash Greatness in Others*. New York, NY: Simon & Schuster, 2022.

Crossan, Mary, Daina Mazutis, Gerard Seijts, and Jeffrey Gandz. "Developing Leadership Character in Business Programs." *Academy of Management Learning & Education* 12 (June 1, 2013): 285-305.

Crossan, Mary, Dusya Vera, and Len Nanjad. "Transcendent Leadership: Strategic Leadership in Dynamic Environments." *The Leadership Quarterly* 19 (October 1, 2008): 569-581.

Daft, Richard L. *The Leadership Experience.* 6th ed. Stamford, CT: Cengage Learning, 2014.

Dahl, Robert A. "The Concept of Power." *Behavioral Science* 2, no. 3 (1957): 201-215.

Damazio, Frank. *The Making of a Leader.* Portland, OR: City Bible Publishing, 1988.

Daniel, Diann. "Soft Skills for CIOs and Aspiring CIOs: Four Ways to Boost Your Emotional Intelligence." *CIO.* June 25, 2007. https://www.cio.com/article/274930/relationship-building-networking-soft-skills-for-cios-and-aspiring-cios-four-ways-to-boost-your-emo.html.

Douglas, J. D., and Merrill C. Tenney. *Zondervan Illustrated Bible Dictionary.* Edited by Moisés Silva. Illustrated ed. Grand Rapids, MI: Zondervan Academic, 2011.

Duguid, Iain M. *The NIV Application Commentary: Ezekiel.* 4th ed. Grand Rapids, MI: Zondervan Academic, 1999.

Elwell, Walter A., ed. *Baker Encyclopedia of the Bible.* Vols. 1 and 2. Grand Rapids, MI: Baker Publishing Group, 1988.

Fee, Gordon. *The First Epistle to the Corinthians.* The New International Commentary on the New Testament. Rev ed. Grand Rapids, MI: Eerdmans Publishing Co., 2014.

Fitzmeyer, Joseph A. *The Gospel According to Luke I-IX: Introduction, Translation, and Notes.* 1st ed. Garden City, NY: Doubleday & Co., 1982.

Forrest, Benjamin, and David Nemitz. "Toward a Biblical Theology of Leadership: Shepherds and Servants on Behalf of the King." In *Biblical Leadership: Theology for the Everyday Leader,* edited by Benjamin

Forrest and Chet Roden. Grand Rapids, MI: Kregel Academic, 2017.

Forrest, Benjamin, and Chet Roden, eds. *Biblical Leadership: Theology for the Everyday Leader.* Grand Rapids, MI: Kregel Academic, 2017.

———. "Introducing 'The' Biblical Foundations of Leadership." In *Biblical Leadership: Theology for the Everyday Leader.* Grand Rapids, MI: Kregel Academic, 2017.

Foster, Richard J. *Celebration of Discipline: The Path to Spiritual Growth Special 20th Anniversary Edition.* San Francisco, CA: HarperSanFrancisco, 2000.

———. *Prayer: Finding the Heart's True Home.* San Francisco, CA: HarperSanFrancisco, 1992.

Fretheim, Terence E. *Jeremiah.* Macon, GA: Smyth & Helwys Publishing, Inc., 2018.

Gleeson, Brian. "The Mission of the Kingdom of God: Ultimate Source of Meaning, Value and Energy for Jesus." *Australasian Catholic Record* 93, no. 3 (July 2016): 326-339.

Goleman, Daniel. "What Makes a Leader?" *Harvard Business Review*, January 1, 2004. https://hbr.org/2004/01/what-makes-a-leader.

Grudem, Wayne. *Systematic Theology: An Introduction to Biblical Doctrine.* 2nd ed. Grand Rapids, MI: Zondervan Academic, 2020.

Gryboski, Michael. "'Pandemic of Narcissism': Seminaries Respond to the Evangelical Church Leadership Crisis." *The Christian Post.* October 9, 2021. https://www.christianpost.com/news/seminaries-respond-to-the-evangelical-church-leadership-crisis.html.

Guinness, Os. "Church Growth—Success At What Price?" *Ligonier Ministries.* April 1, 1992. https://www.ligonier.org/learn/articles/church-growthsuccess-at-what-price/.

Gunter, Nathan H. "For the Flock: Impetus for Shepherd Leadership in John 10." *The Journal of Applied Christian Leadership* 10, no. 1 (2016): 8-18.

Harvey, Robert, and Philip H. Towner. *2 Peter & Jude*. Downers Grove, IL: IVP Academic, 2009.

Hemphill, John K. "Situational Factors in Leadership." *Ohio State University. Bureau of Educational Research Monograph* 32 (1949): 5-6.

Hill, Andrew E., and John H. Walton. *A Survey of the Old Testament*. 3rd ed. Grand Rapids, MI: Zondervan Academic, 2009.

Hirsh, Jacob B., Adam D. Galinsky, and Chen-Bo Zhong. "Drunk, Powerful, and in the Dark: How General Processes of Disinhibition Produce Both Prosocial and Antisocial Behavior." *Perspectives on Psychological Science: A Journal of the Association for Psychological Science 6*, no. 5 (September 2011): 415-427.

House, Paul R. *Old Testament Theology*. Downers Grove, IL: IVP Academic, 2018.

James, Meredith. "Contextual Engagement I Final Paper: The Kingdom of God." Southeastern University, 2021.

———. "Contextual Study of the Ministry Challenge: Foundational Aspects of Kingdom Ministry Leadership." Southeastern University, 2022.

Jobes, Karen H. *1, 2, and 3 John*. Edited by Clinton E. Arnold. Grand Rapids, MI: Zondervan Academic, 2014.

Kaiser Jr., Walter C. "The 'Shepherd' as a Biblical Metaphor: Leadership in Psalm 23." In *Biblical Leadership: Theology for the Everyday Leader*, edited by Benjamin K. Forrest and Chet Roden. Grand Rapids, MI: Kregel Academic, 2017.

Kaplan, Abraham. "Power in Perspective." In *Power and Conflict in Organizations*, edited by Robert L. Kahn and Elise Boulding. London, England: Tavistock, 1964.

Keener. Craig S. *The IVP Bible Background Commentary: New Testament*. Westmont, IL: InterVarsity Press, 1994.

———. *Matthew*. IVP New Testament Commentary Series. Westmont, IL: IVP Academic, 1997.

Keener, Craig S., and John H. Walton, eds. *NIV Cultural Backgrounds Study Bible: Bringing to Life the Ancient World of Scripture*. Special ed. Grand Rapids, MI: Zondervan, 2016.

Keller, W. Phillip. *A Shepherd Looks at Psalm 23*. Grand Rapids, MI: Zondervan, 1970.

Kidner, Derek. *Psalms 1-72 An Introduction & Commentary*. Downers Grove, IL: InterVarsity Press, 1973.

———. *Psalms 73-150*. Downers Grove, IL: IVP Academic, 2009.

Kinnison, Quentin P. "Shepherd or One of the Sheep: Revisiting the Biblical Metaphor of the Pastorate." *Journal of Religious Leadership* 9, no. 1 (Spring 2010): 59-91.

Klett, Leah MarieAnn. "Crisis in Church Leadership: How Celebrity Pastors Can Avoid Failing the Fame Test." *The Christian Post*. October 10, 2021. https://www.christianpost.com/news/how-christian-celebrities-can-avoid-failing-the-fame-test.html.

Kouzes, James M., and Barry Z. Posner. *Credibility: How Leaders Gain and Lose It, Why People Demand It*. San Francisco, CA: Jossey-Bass, 1993.

———. *The Leadership Challenge: How to Make Extraordinary Things Happen in Organizations*. 6th ed. Hoboken, NJ: Jossey-Bass, 2017.

Krasikova, Dina V., Stephen G. Green, and James M. LeBreton. "Destructive Leadership: A Theoretical Review, Integration, and Future Research Agenda." *Journal of Management* 39, no. 5 (July 1, 2013): 1308-1338.

Kruse, Colin G. *2 Corinthians*. Vol. 8. Westmont, IL: IVP Academic, 2015.

Kye, Jae Kwang. "Principles from Jesus Christ's Life That Inform a Biblical Perspective on Servant Leadership." 한국기독교신학논총 72 (December 2010): 263-288.

Ladd, George Eldon. *Gospel of the Kingdom: Scriptural Studies in the Kingdom of God*. Grand Rapids, MI: Eerdmans Publishing Co., 1990.

Lane, William L. *The Gospel According to Mark: The English Text With Introduction, Exposition, and Notes.* 2nd rev. ed. Grand Rapids, MI: Eerdmans Publishing Co., 1974.

Laniak, Timothy S. *Shepherds After My Own Heart: Pastoral Traditions and Leadership in the Bible.* Downers Grove, IL: InterVarsity Press, 2006.

Lewis, C. S. *Mere Christianity.* San Francisco, CA: HarperOne, 2015.

Liden, Robert C., and John Antonakis. "Considering Context in Psychological Leadership Research." *Human Relations* 62, no. 11 (November 1, 2009): 1587-1605.

Lloyd-Jones, Martyn. *The Kingdom of God.* First ed. Wheaton, IL: Crossway, 2010.

Longman III, Tremper, David E. Garland, Walter L. Liefeld, David W. Pao, Robert H. Mounce, and Richard N. Longenecker. *Expositor's Bible Commentary.* Vol. 10, *Luke-Acts.* Rev. ed. Grand Rapids, MI: Zondervan Academic, 2007.

Longman III, Tremper. *Psalms: An Introduction and Commentary.* Downers Grove, IL: IVP Academic, 2014.

———, ed. *The Baker Illustrated Bible Dictionary.* Illustrated ed. Grand Rapids, MI: Baker Books, 2013.

Luter, A. Boyd, and Nicholas Dodson. "Matured Discipleship: Leadership in the Synoptics and Acts." In *Biblical Leadership,* edited by Benjamin Forrest and Chet Rodin, 334-37. Grand Rapids, MI: Kregel Academic, 2017.

Marshall, I. Howard. *Acts: An Introduction and Commentary.* Tyndale New Testament Commentaries. Downers Grove, IL: IVP Academic, 2008.

———. *The Gospel of Luke.* The New International Greek Testament Commentary. American ed. Grand Rapids, MI: Eerdmans Publishing Co., 1978.

Martyr, Justin. *The First Apology of Justin Martyr: An Early Christian Writing.* Orlando, FL: GodSounds, Inc., 2017.

Mathetes. *Epistle to Diognetus*. Translated by Alexander Roberts and James Donaldson. Buffalo, NY: The Christian Literature Company, 1885.

Maxwell, John C. *The 21 Irrefutable Laws of Leadership: Follow Them and People Will Follow You*. Nashville, TN: Thomas Nelson, 1998.

Mayer, John D., Peter Salovey, and David Caruso. "Models of Emotional Intelligence." In *Handbook of Intelligence*, edited by R. J. Sternberg, 396-420. Cambridge, United Kingdom: Cambridge University Press, 2000.

Mayhue, Richard L. "Authentic Spiritual Leadership." *The Master's Seminary Journal* 22, no. 2 (2011): 213-224.

McCracken, Brett. *Hipster Christianity: When Church and Cool Collide*. Grand Rapids, MI: Baker Books, 2010.

McGrath, Alister E. *Christian Theology: An Introduction*. 6th ed. Chichester, West Sussex: John Wiley & Sons Ltd., 2017.

McKnight, Scot, and Laura Barringer. *A Church Called Tov: Forming a Goodness Culture That Resists Abuses of Power and Promotes Healing*. Carol Stream, IL: Tyndale Elevate, 2020.

McNeal, Reggie. *The Present Future: Six Tough Questions for the Church*. San Francisco, CA: Jossey-Bass, 2003.

Meyer, F. B. *Inherit the Kingdom: Meditations on the Sermon on the Mount*. Wheaton, IL: Victor Books, 1985.

Milne, Bruce. *The Message of John*. Assumed First ed. Downers Grove, IL: IVP Academic, 1993.

Moltmann, Jürgen. "Jesus And The Kingdom of God." *The Asbury Journal* 48, no. 1 (January 1, 1993). https://place.asburyseminary.edu/asburyjournal/vol48/iss1/2.

Morris, Leon L. *1 Corinthians*. Downers Grove, IL: IVP Academic, 2008.

———. *Luke: An Introduction and Commentary*. Tyndale New Testament Commentaries. Illustrated ed. Downers Grove, IL: IVP Academic, 2008.

Munsil, Tracy. "US Christians Embrace Secularism in 'Post-Christian' America." *Cultural Research Center Arizona Christian University*.

October 6, 2020. https://www.arizonachristian.edu/2020/10/06/ us-christians-embrace-secularism-in-post-christian-america/.

Myra, Harold, and Marshall Shelley. *The Leadership Secrets of Billy Graham.* Grand Rapids, MI: Zondervan, 2008.

Northouse, Peter G. *Leadership: Theory and Practice.* 8th ed. Thousand Oaks, CA: SAGE Publications, Inc., 2019.

Nouwen, Henri J. M. *Out of Solitude: Three Meditations on the Christian Life.* Rev. ed. Notre Dame, IN: Ave Maria Press, 2004.

———. *The Way of the Heart: Desert Spirituality and Contemporary Ministry.* New York, NY: HarperCollins, 1981.

Origen. *The Complete Works of Origen.* Translated by Philip Schaff. Omaha, NE: Patristic Publishing, 2017.

———. *Origen on Prayer.* Edited by William Curtis. Chicago, IL: Letcetera Publishing, 2015.

Ortberg, John. "What Does God Think of Entertainment?" *CT Pastors.* September 27, 2019. https://www.christianitytoday.com/pastors/2011/spring/whatdoesgodthink.html.

Petersen, Douglas. "Kingdom Rules: Upside-down Discipleship." *Asian Journal of Pentecostal Studies* 16, no. 1 (January 2013): 31-50.

Peterson, Eugene H. *The Pastor: A Memoir.* Reprint ed. San Francisco, CA: HarperOne, 2012.

Rost, Joseph C. *Leadership for the Twenty-First Century.* Westport, CT: Praeger, 1993.

Rost, Joseph C., and Richard A. Barker. "Leadership Education in Colleges: Toward a 21st Century Paradigm," *The Journal of Leadership Studies* 7, no. 1 (2000): 3-12.

Salancik, Gerald R., and Jeffrey Pfeffer. "The Bases and Use of Power in Organizational Decision Making: The Case of a University." *Administrative Science Quarterly* 19, no. 4 (1974): 453-473.

Sanders, J. Oswald. *Spiritual Leadership: Principles of Excellence For Every Believer.* Reissue ed. Chicago, IL: Moody Publishers, 2017.

Scazzero, Peter. *Emotionally Healthy Discipleship: Moving from Shallow Christianity to Deep Transformation*. Grand Rapids, MI: Zondervan, 2021.

———. *The Emotionally Healthy Leader: How Transforming Your Inner Life Will Deeply Transform Your Church, Team, and the World*. Illustrated ed. Grand Rapids, MI: Zondervan, 2015.

Seijts, Gerard. *Good Leaders Learn: Lessons from Lifetimes of Leadership*. 1st ed. New York, NY: Routledge, 2013.

Seijts, Gerard, Jeffrey Gandz, Mary Crossan, and Mark Reno. "Character Matters: Character Dimensions' Impact on Leader Performance and Outcomes." *Organizational Dynamics* 44 (2015): 65-74.

Senior, Donald. *Jesus: A Gospel Portrait*. Mahwah, NJ: Paulist Press, 1992.

Shelton, James B. *Mighty in Word & Deed: The Role of the Holy Spirit in Luke-Acts*. Eugene, OR: Wipf and Stock, 2000.

Smith, Steven W. "Jesus Christ, The Good to Great Shepherd." *Southwestern Journal of Theology* 56, no. 1 (Fall 2013): 53-63.

Sosik, John J., William A. Gentry, and Jae Uk Chun. "The Value of Virtue in the Upper Echelons: A Multisource Examination of Executive Character Strengths and Performance." *The Leadership Quarterly* 23 (2012): 367-382.

Sosler, Alex. "Love in the Ordinary: Leadership in the Gospel of John." *The Journal of Applied Christian Leadership* 11, no. 2 (2017): 10-16.

Spencer, F. Scott. *Gospel of Luke and Acts of the Apostles*. Nashville, TN: Abingdon Press, 2008.

St. Augustine. *Sermo 46*. 1-2, n.d.

Stacy, Robert Wayne. "Following Jesus in the Kingdom of God: Leadership in the Synoptic Gospels." In *Biblical Leadership*, edited by Benjamin Forrest and Chet Roden. Grand Rapids, MI: Kregel Academic, 2017.

Stedman, Ray C., Haddon W. Robinson, and Grant R. Osborne. *Hebrews*. IVP New Testament Commentary Series. Downers Grove, IL: IVP Academic, 1992.

Stefanovic, Ranko. "The Meaning and Message of the Beatitudes in the Sermon on the Mount." *Journal of the Adventist Theological Society.* January 1, 2015. https://works.bepress.com/ranko_stefanovic/33/.

Stogdill, Ralph Melvin. *Handbook of Leadership: A Survey of Theory and Research.* New York, NY: Free Press, 1974.

Stott, John. *The Letters of John.* Tyndale New Testament Commentaries. Reprint ed. Downers Grove, IL: IVP Academic, 2009.

———. *The Message of Ephesians.* The Bible Speaks Today. Downers Grove, IL: IVP Academic, 1984.

———. *The Message of Galatians.* The Bible Speaks Today. Westmont, IL: IVP, 1968.

———. *Christian Counter-Culture: The Message of the Sermon on the Mount.* Westmont, IL: InterVarsity Press, 1978.

Stowell, Joseph M. *Redefining Leadership: Character-Driven Habits of Effective Leaders.* Grand Rapids, MI: Zondervan, 2017.

Sturm, Rachel E., and Lucas Monzani. "Power and Leadership." In *The Nature of Leadership*, edited by John Antonakis and David V. Day. 3rd ed. Thousand Oaks, CA: SAGE Publications, Inc., 2017.

Taylor, John B. *Ezekiel: An Introduction and Commentary.* Tyndale Old Testament Commentaries. Reprint ed. Downers Grove, IL: IVP Academic, 2009.

Tenney, Merrill C., and Moisés Silva. *The Zondervan Encyclopedia of the Bible.* Vol. 5, Q-Z. Grand Rapids, MI: Zondervan, 2009.

Treat, Jeremy R. *Seek First: How the Kingdom of God Changes Everything.* Grand Rapids, MI: Zondervan, 2019.

Tripp, Paul David. *Dangerous Calling: Confronting the Unique Challenges of Pastoral Ministry.* First ed. Wheaton, IL: Crossway, 2012.

———. *Lead: 12 Gospel Principles for Leadership in the Church.* Wheaton, IL: Crossway, 2020.

Ward, Benedicta, ed. *The Desert Fathers: Sayings of the Early Christian Monks.* Rev. ed. London, England: Penguin Classics, 2003.

Watson, JB, Jr., and Walter H. Scalen Jr. "'Dining with the Devil': The Unique Secularization of American Evangelical Churches." *International Social Science Review* 83, no. 3/4 (2008): 171-180.

Wilkes, C. Gene, and Calvin Miller. *Jesus on Leadership: Timeless Wisdom on Servant Leadership.* Wheaton, IL: Tyndale House Publishers, Inc., 1998.

Williamson, Thad. "The Good Society and the Good Soul: Plato's Republic on Leadership." *The Leadership Quarterly* 19, no. 4 (2008): 397.

Wimber, John, and Kevin Springer. *Kingdom Living: Growing in the Character of Christ.* London, England: Hodder & Stoughton Religious, 1988.

Wolfe, Alan. *The Transformation of American Religion: How We Actually Live Our Faith.* New York: Free Press, 2003.

Wright, Walter C. *Relational Leadership: A Biblical Model for Leadership Service.* Carlisle, England: Paternoster, 2000.

Youssef, Michael. *The Leadership Style of Jesus: How to Make a Lasting Impact.* Eugene, OR: Harvest House Publishers, 2013.

ACKNOWLEDGMENTS

This book has been a labor of love, a journey of faith, and a testament to God's guidance every step of the way. It is the result of years of learning, refining, and seeking His wisdom, and I am deeply grateful to those who have walked alongside me through this process.

To my family—Tim and Grant—your unwavering love and prayers have been my anchor, and your encouragement has provided a steady foundation through every stage of this endeavor.

I am deeply grateful to Dr. Sam Hemby, whose wisdom, mentorship, and example of Christ-centered leadership have profoundly influenced not only my ministry but also my life.

Above all, I give glory and honor to God, the true author of this book. He intricately wove its message together, guiding every word and shaping every thought. My prayer is that this book serves as a source of encouragement, challenge, and inspiration—calling pastors and ministry leaders to embrace kingdom leadership with humility, integrity, and boldness.

www.ingramcontent.com/pod-product-compliance
Lightning Source LLC
Chambersburg PA
CBHW021143130626
46554CB00005B/1640